D1713675

Heartbeat from Heaven

Prayer and Praise Unleashed Miracles for My Dying Son

Marcia McGrath Cater

This book is a memoir. It reflects the author's present recollections of her experiences over a period of time. Some events have been compressed, some of the messages have been altered for formatting purposes, and some dialogue has been re-created.

First printing, 2022

ISBN 9798842874347

ENDORSEMENTS

In one moment, a family can be turned upside down. That's exactly what happened to the Caters when their son experienced sudden cardiac arrest and was dead for more than 30 minutes. This gripping story will walk you through the incredible journey they faced with hope, faith, and belief. *Heartbeat from Heaven* is an amazing book that will show you that God still does miracles today, even in the most difficult moments of our lives! *Heartbeat from Heaven* shows us that anything is possible with God and the promises we find throughout the Bible!

– Jason Noble
Real-life pastor behind the character in the film *Breakthrough*, author of *Breakthrough to Your Miracle*, and motivational speaker.

The book that you hold in your hand contains a life-changing story of prayer, hope, worship, and waiting. In a moment, the heart of my healthy 14-year-old cousin suddenly stopped. From the first phone call asking for us to mobilize people to pray, through the many weeks of prayer and waiting, I was astonished by the childlike faith of parents who resolved to trust the One who is worthy of it all, even when it appeared all was lost. The words in this book come straight from that journey. My faith was stretched and my life was changed as I read them then. I pray the same for you as you read them now.

– Brad McKoy
Author of *Culture of the Few*

Be prepared to read an amazing story of how God worked all things together to bring a young man from death to life. I might be tempted to disbelieve some of what is written here if I didn't know the honesty and simple faith of John and Marcia Cater, having been their pastor for 18 years, and remembering well their son's unlikely birth. Marcia shows the skills of a newspaper writer, giving us the *who*, *what*, *when*, and *where* of the story. There is no embellishment, as God's majesty and mystery require none.

Two things that stood out in this story are, first, the importance of God's church. The Caters didn't face this battle alone, but as part of a loving and powerful body of believers. Second, how worship music was a daily source of sustenance for this arduous journey.

This miracle did not come quick and easy. It required endurance in the midst of disappointment. It's a story that will give hope to those still in the waiting phase of faith. Take heart. God can work all things together for your good.

– John K. Smith
Retired pastor and author of
Rublev's Trinity: An Ancient Painting, an Awesome God, and You.

For the healthcare professional, *Heartbeat from Heaven* is an eye-opener that tells the human story of life and death from the enlightening view-point of victims of cardiac arrest and their families. Written with the moving words of a mother who saw her healthy son 'die' in front of her, Christian's story is a powerful tale of hope, faith, and survival...

– Samir Saba, MD
Cardiologist

For from You are all things
And to You are all things
You deserve the glory

From "Worthy of it All"
by David Brymer and Ryan Hall

With gratitude to God
and for His glory

and

In loving memory of
Samuel Joseph Starcher

FOREWORD

I've had the wonderful privilege of knowing Christian Cater for six years. My son, whose name is also Christian, played on the same basketball team with Christian for five years, and I also had the honor of being one of Christian's basketball coaches for two seasons. I found Christian to be a mild-mannered young man and soon realized that he had been raised in a godly home by his impeccable, Christlike behavior. From our first practice on the court, it was evident that he was a gifted young man in basketball, but I was most impressed by his honor and humility that he displayed toward his coaches and the other players on the team. As I watched him year after year, he not only grew in his acquired basketball skills, but also in Christlike character.

I remember the morning when Christian collapsed at his home, and we received several text messages from other parents about his condition. My wife and I joined together, along with our church congregation, in prayer, believing God for a miracle. I remember asking the Lord how this could happen to a young man who seemed so healthy and vibrant. Little did we know that the Miracle Maker was about to perform one of His greatest miracles of all time.

This book that you are about to read describes God's providence and grace, the faith of Christian's parents, and the calling of God upon a young man's life. Our faith is measured by what can stop us. This amazing story reveals the faith of a family and their friends who could not stop believing that God would show up on behalf of this young man. Regardless of negative reports or the physical evidence of Christian's condition, the family's unrelenting faith produced a miracle that needed to be penned in this book, entitled *Heartbeat from Heaven*. Behind the glory is always a story, and Marcia, Christian's mother, needed to write this account to fuel the faith of the readers that nothing is impossible with our God!

It's evident that Christian is chosen for greatness. The calling upon his life is enormous, therefore it was impossible for Christian to leave the planet since his assignment was not finished. The reader of this book will be admonished that all things work together for good to those who love God and are called according to His purpose. Anyone facing a crucible will be encouraged by reading this book because it will build your faith, restore hope, and empower you to believe that there is a better day beyond the crisis. I so look forward to watching Christian fulfill his destiny in Christ in the coming years and to hear of the lives he will impact as a result of this powerful testimony.

I encourage you to not only read this book, but to share it with others because miracles beget miracles in God's kingdom. So, get ready to be encouraged and soar to a new level of faith as you read this miraculous testimony in *Heartbeat from Heaven*. Enjoy!

Dr. Mark Kauffman
Senior Pastor of Jubilee Ministries
Founder of International Network of Kingdom Leaders
CEO of Christian Chamber of Commerce of Western Pennsylvania

Left: Days before his collapse,
Christian attends his first Homecoming dance.

Right: Still the picture of health, about 32 hours before his heart stops,
Christian's soccer team wins the championship.

CHAPTER 1

On that fateful October morning, my 14-year-old son, Christian, was on top of the world. He recently had acquired his first cell phone and attended his first Homecoming dance, and, most important to him, his high school soccer team had captured the championship only 32 hours before.

From birth, Christian was always full of life, bouncing from one sport to another with a sunny grin lighting up his face. I often called him the Energizer Bunny. He was in rare form when he dressed for the Homecoming dance. As his dad played ZZ Top's song "Sharp Dressed Man," Christian cracked us up as he paraded around in his first suit. He strutted through our living room, laughing, wearing sunglasses, tossing his head like a GQ model and posing with the cat. Nobody ever would have guessed that four days later he would be fighting for his life.

On the day that forever changed our lives, he rolled out of bed uncharacteristically early because his soccer team was leaving immediately after school for his first out-of-town tournament and my procrastinator still had some last-minute packing to do.

On a typical school day, Christian didn't drag himself out of bed until after his dad left for work. That morning, John and I were wrapping up our prayer time, which meant John normally would have been out the door in about three minutes.

Just as we said "amen," we heard a loud thud. I wasn't too concerned, assuming Christian had dropped something heavy, and just called him to make sure everything was OK. When he didn't answer, John and I raced to the bathroom to find him face down on the floor, gasping desperately for air. At first, I assumed that he had passed out, but we couldn't get him to regain consciousness. His labored breathing made a horrible sound that, to this day, I wish I could forget. The only thing worse than that sickening sound was when it stopped. Our healthy, athletic son was not breathing.

Even as John and I did all the things we needed to do, the whole situation was completely surreal. It was incomprehensible that someone so young and strong was suddenly struggling to survive.

I immediately called 911, and the operator instructed us to begin CPR. John, who had had some first-aid training, was reluctant to move Christian for fear he had broken his neck when he fell. But thankfully, the operator was adamant. At nearly six feet, three inches tall, Christian was a big boy in a very small bathroom, so maneuvering him gently onto his back was no small challenge.

Once we got Christian into position, John began CPR while I pressed the operator to find out how far away the ambulance was. When he told me where it was coming from, I knew that I could drive from there to our house calmly in about seven minutes, so I expected the ambulance to arrive in about five minutes. Boy, was I mistaken.

CPR instructors will tell you that a person can only perform the life-saving compressions for a few minutes because it's so exhausting. Emergency responders are instructed to take turns every two minutes. But never underestimate the strength and determination that God can give a 59-year-old father with a bad back when his only child is in danger.

While John fought physically to save our son with the CPR, I went to war spiritually. Just the week before, I had learned in a study of Jewish customs that we were in the Jewish month of *Cheshvan*, which is characterized by warring with words. So, I instantly began praying over Christian. I wasn't crying and begging the Lord to spare his life. I was doing spiritual battle, taking authority in Jesus' name to harness the devil and stop him from harming my son.

I don't remember exactly what all I declared and decreed over Christian, but I remember quoting Isaiah 54:17: "No weapon formed against [Christian] shall prosper."

I had a long time to pray before the ambulance arrived. Much longer than I should have. Five minutes came and went. Then ten. At one point, I snapped at the 911 operator, "If you're not going to get an ambulance here, at least pray with me!"

Finally, after the longest 13 minutes of my life, an ambulance showed up.

The emergency responders had their work cut out for them. Just to fit in the bathroom, one of them had to crawl into our bathtub and work from there, while the other perched on the toilet. As quickly as they could, they shocked Christian's heart with an automated external defibrillator (AED). But he did not respond promptly, and they continued laboring over him. At last, his heart temporarily started beating again... after about 30 minutes!

Their next hurdle was carrying Christian down 13 steps to get him to the gurney they'd left on the front porch. Just as they got him situated and started rolling him to the ambulance, his heart stopped again, and they administered the AED a second time.

I didn't learn until two months later that during Christian's most desperate time of need, before we had any chance to send out prayer requests, a precious little girl was interceding for him. Christian's bus stop is one and a half miles from our house, and when he didn't show up that morning, a sweet third grader who gets on at the same stop told her mother, "Maybe Christian is sick today. We should pray for him." And they did.

In these moments, we had no time to analyze why this happened, why Christian, why today? We only had time to react... and pray. But as John and I followed the ambulance to a nearby hospital, I thought of a friend whose soccer-playing son had died in that same hospital, two weeks after his 15th birthday. The day Christian collapsed was exactly two weeks before his 15th birthday. And I wondered if I was going to lose my son there, too.

W hen we arrived at the hospital, I flew out of the car, screaming, "Is he alive?"

One of the emergency medical technicians confirmed that yes, he was, and that they had already summoned a Life Flight helicopter. He said it should arrive in 16 minutes.

When I went to fill out the paperwork, I realized my hands were shaking uncontrollably. I had to use my left hand to steady my right hand so I could sign the forms, and even then, my signature looked like an elderly person had written it.

As the medical staff worked feverishly on Christian, John and I went outside to get cell phone reception so we could finally start alerting friends and family to pray. It was maddening because my hands were still shaking so badly that I had to keep retyping my texts and wasting precious time.

Before long, two police officers walked past us into the hospital, and I told John, "I'll bet they're looking for us." Sure enough, a couple of minutes later they approached us and asked if we were Christian's parents. We weren't the only ones who were wondering what in the world had happened to our son.

While none of us knew at that point what had happened to Christian, we knew what hadn't. The officers were understandably concerned about whether drugs were involved. Once we assured them that Christian flat-out refused to swallow pills and he hated needles, they wished us well and left.

By that time, much longer than 16 minutes had elapsed, with still no helicopter in sight. I was convinced that Christian had died, the ER doctors had canceled the helicopter, and that nobody had the courage to come outside and tell us. So, we ventured into the emergency room.

I was relieved to see the medical staff still working on Christian, although we learned much later that his heart had stopped beating for a third time and had been shocked back into rhythm again.

A doctor who was not actively involved in Christian's care took John and me under his wing. He mentioned a couple of possible diagnoses that matched Christian's symptoms, gave us some tips on driving to UPMC Children's Hospital of Pittsburgh since we weren't allowed to ride in the helicopter, and cautioned us not to race like idiots to the hospital because it would be a long time before he'd be ready for us to see him.

The helicopter finally arrived, and as Christian was wheeled toward the door, I felt compelled to give him something to live for. He had been wheedling us for weeks to have a large outdoor birthday party. But I'd resisted because if the weather didn't cooperate, I knew that his friends wouldn't all fit in our small house. But at that moment, I didn't care. Even though Christian was unconscious, I promised him that if he got better, I'd give him his biggest birthday party ever.

Based on the doctor's wise counsel, John and I opted to run home to grab some necessities before heading to Pittsburgh. We packed phone chargers, a notebook, snacks, and bottles of water, and a couple of days' worth of clothes. We had absolutely no inkling of how many days it would be before all three of us would sleep together in that house again.

On our way to Children's Hospital, John and I made a decision that spared us much agony. We agreed not to use the Internet to research Christian's symptoms or learn more about what he was experiencing. And I'm forever grateful to the paramedics and doctors who didn't tell us the grim outcome they expected since Christian had gone about 30 minutes without a heartbeat. We certainly knew enough to be concerned about possible brain damage, but we had no idea how dire Christian's situation was. If we had Googled how long a person could survive without oxygen, spinalcord.com would have told us that brain cells begin dying at the one-minute mark. At three minutes, lasting brain damage becomes more likely. At ten minutes, even if the brain remains alive, a coma and lasting brain damage are almost inevitable.

In our ignorance, we had a surprisingly calm drive to the hospital, alternately praying and then notifying more family and friends of Christian's urgent need for prayer, and then praying some more.

During that drive, I posted a message on Facebook:

> Christian desperately needs all the prayers he can get. He collapsed this morning and fell hard. He is being life-flighted to Children's Hospital, and he is in an induced coma. He was not breathing for a while, but paramedics shocked him twice and got his heart going again.

At the time, we didn't know about the third shock they'd performed.

My mind wandered back just three nights earlier when I'd stumbled across Psalm 37:4, which says: "Take delight in the Lord, and he will give you the desires of your heart."

Alongside that passage in my Bible, I wrote:

> Lord God, sometime in the next four years, please allow Christian's soccer team to win a championship so he can enjoy the desires of his heart.

Not only had his team won the championship the following night, but Christian scored a goal in a game that, as a freshman, he hadn't even expected to get to play in. Now I wondered if God had answered my prayer so promptly because Christian would never get to play soccer again. Ever.

A ll my calmness vanished when we got to the hospital, where we had never been before. Once we parked the car, we had no idea where to go. The parking garage is on the back side of the hospital, and we couldn't find any people or signs to direct us. It was maddening to be so close and still unable to find Christian.

We eventually stumbled on the front desk, where my frustration only mounted. A nurse had called us during our drive to the hospital to say we were cleared to go straight to the Intensive Care Unit on the fifth floor, specifically noting that the security guards had been notified to allow us through even though we wouldn't have the usual nametags. But the woman at the front desk had her own agenda. Despite my fervent protests, she refused to let us pass without filling out all the paperwork. I didn't know if my son was dead or alive, and I couldn't get past a receptionist!

The only bright spot at that front desk was that two of our pastors were waiting for us there. It sure was comforting to see their familiar faces.

When we finally made it to the fifth floor, I was relieved to learn Christian was still alive. But all our hurrying was for naught, as he was getting a CT scan and then doctors were hooking him up to a myriad of machines, so we weren't allowed to see him for at least an hour. John and I and our growing circle of support, including Christian's youth pastor and one of our dear friends, were ushered into our own private small room to wait. And pray. I still felt the urgent need to wage spiritual warfare on Christian's behalf, declaring and decreeing that he was God's child and binding the devil with the authority we have through Christ.

As we sat in that room, we unknowingly tapped into the lifeline that would carry us through the next month: worship music.

We sang the lullaby by Otis L. McCoy that I sang to Christian as an infant:

> All night, all day
> Angels watching over me, my Lord.
> All night, all day
> Angels watching over me.

We sang "Whom Shall I Fear" by Chris Tomlin, with a chorus that proclaims:

> I know who goes before me
> I know who stands behind
> The God of angel armies
> Is always by my side.

Another chorus we sang, written by Daniel Gardner, says:

> My life is in You, Lord
> My strength is in You, Lord
> My hope is in You, Lord.

As we sang, the Lord strongly impressed on me that we were to continually play praise music in Christian's room to create an atmosphere of peace and healing.

The other significant thing that happened in that small waiting room was that our pastor recommended I use a little journal the hospital provided to record key steps in Christian's journey to recovery. With my degree in journalism, writing was right down my alley, and it gave me something constructive to do. One of my first entries was a statement from Christian's youth pastor, who that morning had been reading Nehemiah 8:10, which says in part that "the joy of the Lord is my strength."

And then I wrote words that I didn't even remember her saying, but which proved prophetic. She said, "People choosing to worship during hardship releases God to give his strength."

Another early entry in that little red journal came from our friend who waited with us. She told how that morning, at almost the exact minute Christian collapsed, she had been listening to a song called "Mary, Did You Know?" When she got to the line that talked about Jesus saving our children, she burst into tears for no apparent reason. She kept replaying it and crying more. Only later did she learn of Christian's ordeal. We absolutely claimed the promise of those lyrics for Christian's healing. That song is particularly special to our family because when Christian was about four months old, he made his stage debut portraying baby Jesus in a music video of it at our church.

W hen John and I finally were allowed to see Christian, a nurse led us through a labyrinth of hallways to the last room in the farthest corner of the Pediatric Intensive Care Unit (PICU), which was wonderfully quiet and private. God mercifully enabled me to look beyond all the medical machinery covering Christian and see only my "little boy." Ordinarily, any mention of blood or medical procedures makes my legs go weak, but I never batted an eyelash at the needles, tubes, and other devices covering every inch of Christian, except the tip of his nose and his right shoulder.

Even though Christian was unconscious, I had read that people can sometimes hear, even if they can't respond. So, we talked to Christian a lot, explaining the best we could what was going on, and always, always, always keeping the conversation in the room positive and uplifting.

By that time, the medical staff had determined that Christian had experienced a sudden cardiac arrest, and they were working to determine what caused it. The first doctor described Christian as "stable but very ill" and a colleague summarized his situation as "very critical; a life-threatening condition." The two biggest concerns were his brain and his heart.

The doctor explained that they were keeping Christian in an induced coma and lowering his body temperature, which would help his brain recover from any trauma. Even if he could breathe on his own, they didn't want him to, so that his body could rest. So, he had machines doing absolutely every function that his own body normally would.

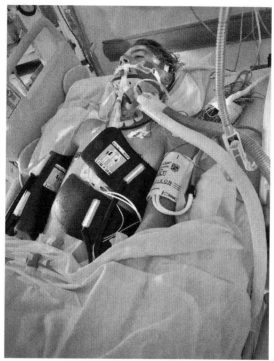

Very early in Christian's care at UPMC Children's Hospital of Pittsburgh.

That doctor, like every medical person we would meet over the next several days, emphasized that there was absolutely no doubt that the CPR that John had performed had saved Christian's life. The CPR kept the blood flowing through Christian's body and that provided oxygen to his vital organs.

A cardiology team explained to us that the ventricles in Christian's heart were not squeezing normally and that the left one was pumping weakly. Although John and I didn't know it at the time, throughout the afternoon, his heart rate numbers worsened.

I learned that day that a sudden cardiac arrest differs from a heart attack, although people often mistakenly use the terms interchangeably. "A heart attack is when blood flow to the heart is blocked, and sudden cardiac arrest is when the heart malfunctions and suddenly stops beating unexpectedly," according to heart.org. "A heart attack is a 'circulation' problem and sudden cardiac arrest is an 'electrical' problem."

Sudden cardiac arrests often occur with no warning signs. They are triggered by an electrical malfunction in the heart that causes an irregular heartbeat called arrhythmia. With its pumping action disrupted, the heart cannot pump blood into the brain, lungs, and other organs. Seconds later, a person loses consciousness and has no pulse. Death occurs within minutes if the victim does not receive treatment, according to "Heart Attack and Sudden Cardiac Arrest Differences" on cpr.heart.org.

The website explained that symptoms of a heart attack may be immediate and intense. More often, though, symptoms start slowly and persist for hours, days, or weeks before a heart attack. Unlike a sudden cardiac arrest, the heart usually does not stop beating during a heart attack.

While John and I were trying to process those differences, a kind nurse cautioned us that we well could go through Post Traumatic Stress Disorder because of Christian's situation. In my naivete, I just stared blankly at her. I'd always believed incorrectly that PTSD was something suffered only by members of the military during battles; it hadn't hit me yet that the medical horror we'd already gone through and those yet to come could produce the same ill effects as fighting in a war. In hindsight, I clearly grasp the parallels. I believe that only our faith in and reliance on God spared us from the nightmare of PTSD, which studies show occurs in one out of three caregivers of sudden cardiac arrest patients.

When we asked one of the doctors how long we should expect Christian to be in the hospital, he estimated two weeks. So, I fully expected Christian to be home in time to celebrate his 15th birthday, exactly two weeks away.

That evening, a couple who we are friends with through Christian's school asked if they could come and pray with us. They arrived toting the first of many gift baskets full of food and drinks, which were a godsend because they eliminated the need for us to leave Christian's room to eat in the hospital cafeteria. While we had been good friends for five years, we'd never prayed aloud together, so I was immensely grateful to hear them praying the same type of warfare prayers I had been saying all day. When they prayed the same Bible verses I'd been clinging to and called for angels to encamp around him, as I'd been singing, their words affirmed my own. They added one more sentiment that I hadn't even thought of, but I readily agreed: they decreed Christian would live to give glory to God out of his situation.

While there's no good time for something like a cardiac arrest, John and I were keenly aware that the timing could've been much, much worse. If Christian had had it while he was sleeping, we never would've known until it was too late. If Christian had collapsed 24 hours later, he would've been with teenage soccer teammates in a hotel room in Ohio, far from the expert care of a Children's Hospital.

Providentially, he collapsed on a Wednesday, which is chapel day at Portersville Christian School, where Christian attended. By 8:30 a.m., the staff and entire junior and senior high were in chapel, interceding with us for Christian's life. Additionally, our church has Wednesday night classes, and Christian's youth pastor and some of his Sunday school teachers used social media to pull together a prayer vigil on his behalf that evening.

I still marvel at how many families from Christian's school, which draws families from a five-county area, found their way to our rural church. Between our church and school families, the sanctuary was full.

Not only did Christian's heart rate numbers improve while that prayer service was going on, but we believe all those prayers, along with hundreds more from friends and family and their prayer networks, laid the groundwork for what happened next.

CHAPTER 2

That first evening, I received a text from another dear friend who ministers prophetically, which means that the Lord speaks through her to give His messages to others. I've watched the Lord use her this way for more than 30 years, so I didn't hesitate to follow her instructions when she wrote:

> I am very concerned for Christian and am praying the healing oil of Jesus touch him from his head to his toe right now. He knows what is needed and will provide Christian with it.

A bit later she texted again:

> Pour some of that healing oil on his head. Just need you to do it. It soothes, smooths the rough, and will heal that head, I believe.

The only problem was that we couldn't find any anointing oil. A couple of friends went on a mission throughout the hospital to find some, and they reported that the only way we could've gotten any was if we'd allowed a priest to come and give Christian last rites. We politely declined because we wanted to speak life, not death, over him. I asked my prophetic friend if we should try using cooking oil, but she said we should use legitimate anointing oil. We had to settle for waiting until the next day when another friend was willing to relay a bottle to us from our pastor's supply.

The following morning, my prophetic friend was flying out of town, but she still managed to text me:

That oil will soothe Christian all over, says the Lord. *I will smooth the rough in his head that needs smoothed and heal him with My hand.* Praise Him. Whoever pours a small amount on his head and gently rubs it over should just repeat, "Jesus, Jesus." Have a peaceful day.

The anointing oil arrived by 10 a.m., but we had to wait until noon for a break in the steady stream of nurses and doctors working over Christian. By that time, Christian's "adopted grandma" had arrived, and it seemed natural for her to join me in anointing him. All of Christian's biological grandparents were in heaven by the time he was in second grade, but the Lord had sent him a bonus Grammy named Esther. She had been with me throughout my pregnancy, at the hospital on the day he was born, and babysat Christian throughout his life. She was undoubtedly Christian's favorite person on the planet because of her intense love for children, her adventurous, childlike nature... and because she rarely told him "no."

We began, as instructed, simply praying the name of Jesus over Christian. But after a while, the Holy Spirit reminded me that, in the Bible, people were anointed for two different reasons: for healing and for dedication to the Lord's service. Even though we had planned only to follow my prophetic friend's instructions, we wound up anointing Christian a second time and praying over specific body parts. For example, we prayed over his feet that the Lord would direct his steps and send Christian wherever He wanted him to go in life, and we prayed over his hands that the Lord would use them to help others in Jesus' name.

When we were finished, I knew we had experienced a powerful prayer time, but I had no idea just how powerful. Esther told me that as I'd prayed, she felt electricity shooting through her body, and God had opened her eyes to see an angel ministering over Christian's head. She described the angel as invisible but visible, very pretty, white, with wings. She said the angel's face was so heavenly that she didn't look much at the rest of her, but said the angel's hand was on Christian's head and her mouth was moving, like she, too, was praying.

When I texted my prophetic friend to let her know we'd finally been able to anoint Christian, I told her that Esther had been there for it, and she replied:

> Oh my goodness! I felt she should be the one to do this. Please tell her! The Lord showed me this, but we were in the air and I couldn't get the message to you. Yes, this is what the Lord wanted exactly. Thank you, Esther!!!!! I actually saw her doing this. Yah!!!!!! Praise God for you, Esther. He needs Esther for such a time as this...

Mercifully, throughout Christian's ordeal, I remained too naïve to realize exactly how severe his injuries could have been. When Esther concurred that she also felt at peace that Christian would be fine, I simply accepted my friends' prophecies and expected him to make a full recovery.

Although we have no way of proving it, I believe Christian's brain was healed when he was anointed, but his body still had a long way to go.

H appily, we learned later that day that his body had taken a big step in the right direction. I had quickly learned that Facebook was the most efficient way to keep family and friends updated on Christian's condition, and my post for Day Two said:

> I have some good news to share with all of Christian's prayer warriors: his left ventricle, which was pumping blood very weakly yesterday, now is in the normal range! Yesterday it was pumping at 26; today it is 60. Normal range is 50 to 65. They have ruled out several possible causes (of the cardiac arrest), but many more tests will be happening in the next few days. His numbers have all been trending well, but the doctors stress to us that he is still in very critical condition, so please continue lifting him up in prayer.

He was anointed with oil today, both for healing and for service to the King of kings and Lord of lords.

Whenever it wouldn't interfere with Christian's medical team, we kept praise and worship music playing in his room, mainly by placing a phone on the pillow next to his ear and playing songs from YouTube. On this day, the lyrics to "In Christ Alone," by Keith Getty and Stuart Townend, really gripped me because I still firmly believed everything going on in Christian's body and our lives was a spiritual battle. So, I hung on to these lyrics:

> *Jesus commands my destiny.*
> *No power of hell, no scheme of man,*
> *Can ever pluck me from His hand.*

By that time, doctors were leaning toward the belief that Christian's cardiac arrest wasn't linked to any disease in his heart. We were told he would likely wind up with a defibrillator implanted in his chest before he left the hospital. Its function would be to automatically shock Christian's heart back into rhythm if it ever went out of whack again.

When the team of doctors and support staff made their daily rounds, John and I were graciously invited to listen in. For the most part, we remained silent and had to ask lots of follow-up questions later to our nurse to figure out what had been said. But one day, the doctors mentioned Christian had fentanyl in his system. Thinking they were saying Christian had ingested it before coming to the hospital, I couldn't help myself from shrieking, "What?!" The doctors all laughed and assured me they had administered the drug to him.

I don't know much about illegal drugs, but I recognized that name from the many newspaper stories I'd read about the opioid epidemic. With great concern that Christian might wind up accidentally addicted, I asked his nurse about it. She assured me of two things: At that time, he was better off with it than without it because medically administered fentanyl was safer than the street drug, and that the hospital knew how to wean him off it when the time was right. I was never comfortable with him receiving it, but she was correct that he eventually was able to get off it without lasting effects.

John and I continued to be grateful for how well Children's Hospital not only cared for our son but cared for us parents as well. Each patient room in the PICU contained a sofa with a trundle, which enabled both of us to stay with Christian around the clock. They also provided us with toiletries and towels for use in showers reserved just for parents. They went above and beyond to make our lives as comfortable as possible under the circumstances.

O n Day Three, Christian was originally scheduled for an MRI of his heart, but doctors ultimately decided it was safer to first warm his body up to normal temperatures, a process that would take 24 hours. He faced many possible complications during his warm-up period.

The highlight of my day came from the soccer tournament in Ohio that Christian was missing. We received three videos: one from his team-mates, one from his coaches, and one from the bus driver/friend who drives his regular bus route and carpools with our family to athletic practices. The videos were chock-full of love, jokes, prayers, and encour-agement.

We were constantly talking to Christian, so it seemed only natural to play the videos for him. Within seconds, his nurse charged into the room, demanding to know what was going on. Her monitor showed that Christian's heart rate and blood pressure both shot up as soon as he started hearing his friends' voices. She told us in no uncertain terms that we needed to stop stimulating him so much, and we understood the staff was trying to keep him calm to facilitate his healing. But in my heart, I was rejoicing... my boy had responded! He couldn't talk and he couldn't move, but he had responded in the only manner he could–with a jump in his vital signs.

I know that social media has many negatives, but it was a lifeline for us from the beginning. My original SOS requesting prayer for Christian garnered 197 comments and was shared 63 times. Within hours, Christian was receiving prayer not just from all over the United States, but from around the world. We were flooded with uplifting scripture verses, song lyrics, and words of encouragement from friends and family, as well as strangers. We were completely humbled; we were nobody special, yet hundreds of people were standing by us. We were grateful that so many people were praying with us, and their kind comments helped carry John and me throughout the ordeal.

Christian was getting to be somewhat of a celebrity. When I called my doctor to order a prescription refill for myself, the receptionist, who did not know me at all, said, "Is it your son who is all over Facebook?" She had seen his name so much on Facebook that when she heard my last name, she put two and two together.

Similarly, Christian's youth pastor was talking to a couple of ladies at a gym. When the youth pastor started to leave, she mentioned she was going to visit one of her church kids, a 14-year-old who had had a cardiac arrest. One of the women responded, "Oh, I know about him from Facebook!"

On the day Christian collapsed, a woman we don't know had been shopping at Costco. While waiting to talk to a manager, she overheard a conversation in which one of our friends mentioned a 14-year-old had had a cardiac arrest. This customer was so touched by the story that she kept praying for Christian throughout the day. When she got home that night, she discovered that our family and she share a mutual friend, who had requested prayer for Christian on Facebook... and she already had been lifting him up.

Word about Christian had spread throughout the soccer tournament as well, and many prayers were being lifted up on our behalf from there.

John and I were especially touched to get word, one by one, that at least six of the Christian schools that our son's soccer team played against during its regular season were praying faithfully for us; two eventually sent him care packages and one took time during its annual soccer banquet to pray for Christian. As competitive as these kids were on the field, they came together in unity for a larger purpose.

I kicked off Day Four with this post on Facebook:

> We all rested well last night. (John joked that he and I must also have been in induced comas.) The warm-up process is going smoothly, and he should be up to normal temperature around 4 p.m. Once he is warm, if his blood pressure remains stable, then they will begin to let him wake up slightly. But they want to keep him mostly asleep in preparation for tests on Monday. If all goes as planned today, they hope to give him a feeding tube this evening so he can start receiving nourishment. He would rather be at Chick-fil-A... but it's a start! John's song for today is "Surrounded" by Michael W. Smith and mine is "To God Be the Glory" by Lou Fellingham. Many thanks for carrying our family through your prayers!!

Meanwhile, out in the real world, the teens in Christian's youth group were gathering to assemble and deliver submarine sandwiches, which they sell periodically to raise money for camps, retreats, and other activities. Christian's customers had ordered 119 subs, and his teen friends and our adult friends rose to the occasion in making his orders and getting them into the right hands. To our knowledge, thanks to a real team effort, all subs were delivered successfully.

Throughout the day, Christian's warm-up went off without a hitch and his nurse throttled back on the medication that was keeping him unconscious. That evening, without any fanfare, a nurse came in and asked Christian if he could open his eyes... and he did! Then, one by one, she held Christian's hands and asked if he could squeeze her hand... and he did! Her next request was for Christian to wiggle the toes on one foot and then the other... and he did!

I was so excited that I jumped up and down, tears of joy streaming down my cheeks, with both hands clamped over my mouth so I didn't cheer out loud. The last time I was that relieved and exultant was when I was pregnant with Christian, and my first ultrasound showed he was alive. I'd already had three miscarriages, and I was bleeding abnormally, so we'd feared we were losing Christian, too. When John and I heard his heartbeat for the first time, it was such a blessed sound that at the end of our appointment, we asked if we could listen to it again.

And now Christian's responses to the nurse were equally momentous. His ability to respond to the nurse's requests was a huge breakthrough because it proved his brain and body both were working and cooperating with each other. Even though he still had a respirator breathing for him, he was laboring hard to breathe on his own, which showed his lungs were working.

As I affirmed in my journal that night, "We trust in the name of the Lord our God!"

On Sunday, Day Five, I shared with our prayer warriors that:

All continues to progress here slowly, but surely. At the moment, Christian is being prepped for a spinal tap. Doctors doubt it will reveal anything; it is just a precaution to rule out several other possible issues. At this time, Monday will be another quiet day of peaceful healing. Tuesday will be the big day. His MRI is rescheduled for an unknown time that day. If all goes well with it, they can begin to remove his breathing tube and start to bring him back to consciousness. I cannot wait!!

All of Christian's readings are good and he is resting comfortably. Doctors did opt to re-paralyze Christian, but this is NOT a bad thing. He was being so active when he was not in the induced coma that they wanted him to be more still. But hear me clearly, it is good that he was able to be that active!! All along, they planned to keep Christian pretty well out of it until he gets the MRI. They brought him out of it yesterday just to test his responses with eyes, hands, and feet. Responses were excellent every time they were tested.

The song for that day was "Our God," by Chris Tomlin, which includes the lyrics:

Our God is greater, our God is stronger
God, You are higher than any other
Our God is Healer, awesome in power
Our God, Our God
And if our God is for us
Then who could ever stop us?
And if our God is with us
Then what can stand against?

In God's divine timing, weeks before Christian collapsed, our church scheduled a rare healing service in which people would share praise reports of past healings. Anyone who needed healing would be invited to receive prayer. In the 33 years that we've attended our church, we'd had a handful of these services. Three weeks earlier, on October 7, the Lord strongly had impressed on me that I was to share a praise at the service. At the time, I assumed I was to share about how God took care of me ten years earlier when I'd been diagnosed with blood clots throughout the lower half of my body.

Within the next two weeks, all hell broke loose in our household. Literally. After about a week of chaos, I recognized that we were in the midst of a spiritual battle–that the devil was attacking us–but I was baffled as to why. Normally, when our family undergoes such attacks, it coincides with some new ministry we're getting involved with, but we had nothing out of the ordinary going on... yet.

Three days after God told me to share at the healing service, I wound up in the hospital. I really believed I was having some type of issue with the blood clots again for the first time in a decade, and I remember thinking on the way to the hospital, "Well, Lord, this might make it a little tricky to share at the healing service." But He had made it so clear that I was to share, I was determined to follow through. Thankfully, it turned out that my pain had nothing to do with blood clots.

Furthermore, testing was able to confirm that my clotting situation hadn't worsened any in the past ten years, a fact that I squirreled away to share at the healing service.

During those two crazy weeks, in addition to my spending three days in the hospital, my car battery died, our seven-month-old microwave gave up the ghost, we were slapped with a $1,500 bill that we were expecting to cost $500, we had to straighten out a banking snafu, and, because of my hospital stay, John and I completely forgot about the show we had tickets to see for our anniversary. To put it all in perspective, at the end of the month, John said that the best day he'd had all month was the day he got his colonoscopy!

During that topsy-turvy time, I hung on to two things:

In the class I was taking on Jewish customs, we were reading *A Time to Advance* by Chuck D. Pierce. In the chapter that described the Jewish month of *Cheshvan*, which includes parts of October and November, Pierce portrayed it as being a time to war with words. He wrote, "Satan wants to get the upper hand, but this is the time to plant your heel on the enemy's plan to transform you into his image. Instead, as you deal with your trials and difficulties through the anointing, you will be changed into Christ's image."

Along with that, the Biblical passage about the armor of God in Ephesians 6:10-20, spoke powerfully to me. It begins, "Be strong in the Lord and in his mighty power." After my own hospital stay, I had felt incredibly weak, both physically and spiritually. But just reading those words and going for a tree-lined walk along a babbling brook rejuvenated me.

The Scripture goes on to say, "Put on the full armor of God, so that you can take your stand against the devil's schemes. For our struggle is not against flesh and blood, but against the rulers, against the authorities, against the powers of this dark world and against the spiritual forces of evil in the heavenly realms." That was a good reminder for me not to get frustrated over all the things going wrong in our household, but to recognize that the devil was behind all of them... and that I was not powerless.

The verses then describe all the weapons I had at my disposal to combat the enemy's attacks: the belt of truth, the breastplate of righteousness, feet fitted with the readiness that comes from the gospel of peace, the shield of faith, the helmet of salvation and the sword of the Spirit, which is the Word of God.

The passage ends with the writer, Paul, saying, "Pray also for me, that whenever I speak, words may be given me so that I will fearlessly make known the mystery of the gospel..." I applied those words to the upcoming healing service and trusted that the Lord would give me whatever words I was to speak.

When the night that I was to share finally arrived, Christian had been in the hospital for five days. It was obvious that the story I was to share was not about blood clots, but about the miracle unfolding in his life. Although his healing was still very much a work in progress, I was able to proclaim the goodness of God to our congregation without ever leaving Christian's hospital room through the marvels of modern technology. I truly don't remember what I said that night, but I trust that they were the words God had intended for me to say when he'd spoken to me three long weeks earlier.

By that time, Christian's soccer team was home from its tournament and two of his teammates who hadn't been able to attend the prayer vigil for him attended the healing service instead. John and I were touched and grateful that one of the young men sat in proxy for Christian while several people prayed again for his continued healing.

During the healing service, our pastor sent John and me a significant text:

> As I am praying, I feel led to tell you to not be surprised if the doctors and tests reveal nothing. The lepers healed by Jesus had no sign of any skin disease. The lame healed never walked with a limp and the dead were raised to full life. Don't be surprised if Christian has no symptoms or issues.

CHAPTER 3

Almost immediately after that healing service, Christian took a turn for the worse. By 4:30 a.m., his blood pressure started fluctuating wildly because something inside of him wasn't regulating it correctly. For the first time since he was hospitalized, he didn't urinate at all during a two-hour stretch. He was supposed to be receiving food through a feeding tube, but he didn't get any all night because of a kink in the line. Every time doctors tried to take Christian off the drug that kept him paralyzed, he got agitated and they were forced to resume it. On top of all that, he developed a bacterial infection from having the breathing tube.

Usually, God had been giving me a song each morning that would carry me through the day. But on that Monday, Day Six, He didn't give me a song until nighttime. "Praise You in This Storm," by Casting Crowns, contains this chorus:

> *I'll praise You in this storm, and I will lift my hands*
> *That You are who You are, no matter where I am*
> *And every tear I've cried, You hold in Your hand*
> *You never left my side, and though my heart is torn*
> *I will praise You in this storm.*

Praising God in the storm was exactly what I needed to do after a draining day. In the wee hours of the night, I slipped alone into a small lounge area with a beautiful view overlooking the city of Pittsburgh. I played various praise songs on my cell phone as God and I worked through some things and He restored my strength. I still believed that Christian would make a full recovery, but I felt I needed to prepare myself in case he didn't. God met me right where I was through the song "Blessings" by Laura Story.

Over and over, I played the song, which includes the lyrics:

'Cause what if Your blessings come through raindrops
What if Your healing comes through tears?
What if a thousand sleepless nights
Are what it takes to know You're near?
What if trials of this life are Your mercies in disguise?
What if my greatest disappointments,
Or the aching of this life,
Is the revealing of a greater thirst this world can't satisfy?
What if trials of this life,
The rain, the storms, the hardest nights,
Are Your mercies in disguise?

After about an hour of "praising in the storm," my peace was restored. I was able to sleep, knowing that whether Christian made a full recovery or not, we would be OK.

While I was writing this book, our pastor said in one of his sermons, "Testing is an opportunity for trust and relationships to be made stronger." Even in the midst of all the chaos and uncertainty, I felt like my relationships with the Lord and my husband had never been deeper. I felt incredibly close to both of them, and those bonds gave me peace. As strange as this sounds, it was easier to draw near to God while I was in the hospital than at home for two reasons. I didn't have the day-in, day-out household chores to distract me from spending time with the Lord, and Christian's recovery was so far out of my control that I had no other recourse but to pray and trust God. In the months since Christian's hospitalization, I've many times thought of the deep sense of God's presence I experienced there, and wistfully wished for a way to recapture it.

My Facebook update for Tuesday, Day Seven, said:

Monday was a day of disappointments. The most frustrating for this mama's heart is that the MRI got pushed back until Wednesday. It was not for any medical reason, but because the schedule for today was full, even though we have known since last Friday that he was to receive it today. (Remember, they cannot take out his breathing tube until after the MRI, so I will not hear my baby's sweet voice for a full day longer.)

Christian also started running a fever yesterday, and now they say he has pneumonia. The nurses are not too excited about that, but to me, it seems like a step backward.

We also learned that Christian will likely be moved to the cardiac intensive care sometime today. I have no doubt that he will receive the same excellent care there that he has received here in PICU. But we have been warned that the rooms there are much smaller, which will make it challenging for John and me to continue to sleep in the same room with him. Plus, we have bonded with the nurses and doctors on this floor, and have had opportunity to minister to other parents who are walking their own heartbreaking journeys, some of which are significantly worse than Christian's.

We never got transferred to the cardiac unit, which enabled us to continue our ministry in the PICU. I'd heard the expression that "there are no atheists in foxholes," but I decided the same is true of parents with very sick children. Though we came from varied backgrounds, ranging from Amish to unchurched, not one parent we offered to pray with turned us down.

We were able to pray with one mother whose two sons both had contracted a virus; one recovered normally, but his toddler brother was fighting for his life. This mom, like many others, was navigating the medical maze alone because her husband had to stay at home in West Virginia with their older son. After some days that were touch-and-go and a surgery that was so risky that one doctor refused to do it, the little guy responded and began to improve.

Another inspirational mom we met was no stranger to the PICU. Her son has severe medical problems that require frequent hospitalizations. Her husband also was at home, a few hours away, with their other child. I couldn't imagine what it was like for these women to be all alone, going through the stress and uncertainty and having to make decisions themselves, so John and I spent as much time with them as we could. I'll never forget this mother's comment, without any bitterness, "The difference between our boys is that yours will eventually walk out of here; someday, mine will come here and he won't leave."

I went into that hospital so naïve, assuming that the children were mostly all there from natural causes. But I soon learned how sadly wrong I was. Police visits were quite common because of the number of children who were hospitalized because of criminal activity.

We were able to pray with one couple whose infant son was shaken so badly by a babysitter that brain damage was feared, and one woman whose grandbaby overdosed on Tylenol administered by a babysitter.

Our stay was also eye-opening regarding the number of children who were life-flighted to the hospital daily. One time, we watched one helicopter circle and wait while another one unloaded its precious cargo.

Every time we heard a helicopter coming in, we stopped to pray for that child and its parents, understanding full well what they were going through. One morning, a request came through our church's prayer chain for a boy who had gotten hit by a car the night before and was life-flighted to Children's Hospital. I was able to assure the friend who'd requested prayer that we had been praying for him even before she asked for it. We later met that boy's parents and were able to tell them the same thing.

My heart went out to all the parents who lived so far from the hospital that they had no support system of family and friends to care for their needs as they cared for their children. John and I were so overwhelmingly blessed by all the help we received that I sometimes felt guilty. Our guardian angels visited daily, bought us meals, brought us homemade food, sent gifts, donated money to help with extra expenses, even did our laundry, and cleaned our house. We couldn't possibly have had more wonderful support and encouragement.

One perfect example of that support was the incredible text we received that day from an amazing friend, which we wound up reading to Christian many times, and it became an anchor for us all throughout his hospital stay. It said:

> This morning I was praying for you, and I gathered up in my mind a picture of you, Christian, and Jesus sitting in a canoe, not too much bigger than the two of you could fit. You were in the middle of a great big lake. It was peaceful and calm and so beautiful. Now, Christian, I know you may prefer to kayak, but Jesus can't sit next to you in that, and He wants to be beside you to wrap His arms around you, to look into your eyes to tell you His story and for you to be able to look at Him to focus.

> Jesus was telling you His story about being out on the water with His disciples and that great big storm came rolling through. Do you remember how scared His disciples were about that storm? And what was Jesus doing? He was sleeping! He had no fear. Jesus knew where the power of the storm laid, in Him. And then He walked up and called out to the storm, "Quiet! Be still!" And the storm stopped, the wind, the rain, all of it obeyed Jesus' command. And it became calm again.

> I think Jesus wants you to know that right now, your body is calm, the medicine is keeping it still. But it's time to let that part of your story end and to take up the next part. It will mean that you will feel a storm going on inside of you. There may be fear that wants to rise up around you; there may be many feelings that you want to get out of the place you are. Know that the disciples felt that way. But Jesus never did. He sat and He stilled.

Now buddy, you showed us amazingly on Saturday that you CAN hear and respond to commands. Jesus wants for you to picture Him. Can you use your mind to pull up the canoe on the lake and just the two of you? He wants you to speak the word peace over your body, think peace, repeat peace, over and over again. We will all do it with you to help you, to bring angels of peace to calm all around you. Jesus will calm the storm within you; just focus your eyes on Him and allow His peace to come over you.

Right now, you have things attached to you that will feel funny, may even hurt or be uncomfortable a little bit, but when you come off the medicine, all of that will be addressed. You are wonderfully cared for. If you allow the storm to move you, it can disrupt those things attached to you. They need to stay another day.

Do you know that after the storm, Jesus and His disciples moved on from the lake and went about healing? The storm in your body is going to move you to the next thing God is calling you to. So, today, see Jesus, look into His eyes, and let peace reside over you, His peace. Jesus is calm in this because He knows where the power for peace is from: Him.

We are all praying for your body to have peace. This is an important step on your journey, and Jesus is right beside you. He wants to comfort you when you are upset, fill you with truth, and guide you through the storm. Buddy, we all love you so much! We are speaking peace for you and trusting that Jesus, our peace, heaven's peace, is calling the storm to be still within you.

The next day, October 31, began our second week in the hospital. Thankfully, this Halloween held all treats and no tricks for us.

After six days of endless waiting for the MRI of Christian's heart and neck, suddenly things kicked into high gear. His MRI had been scheduled for mid-afternoon, but his nurses got a call at about 8:30 a.m. to see if they could get him ready for a 9 a.m. opening. They worked feverishly to make all his medications and machines movable, which was no small challenge. With two nurses working as fast as they safely could, it took about 45 minutes to get Christian mobile.

We had been somewhat concerned about how Christian's body would handle anesthesia since he had never had it before, but they were able to perform the MRIs without anesthesia.

The MRIs were worth the wait. Results of the one on his neck were so good that they were able to remove his neck collar because they showed no damage to his vertebrae. They were also able to disconnect the EEG sensors from his head because the risk of seizures was no longer a concern. Those two improvements created more space, both on his body and in his room. The MRI of his heart showed no obvious cause of his cardiac arrest, and since there was no evidence of problems with the heart muscle, doctors continued to believe electrical issues that caused arrhythmia were the prime culprit. One doctor told us firmly that Christian would not leave the hospital without having a defibrillator implanted. But God had other plans.

Early on, I had asked one of Christian's nurses what I should ask his prayer warriors to focus on. One of the things she'd specifically mentioned was that doctors would order all MRIs he might need all at the same time. Sadly, that did not happen. We no more than got the results of his first two MRIs than the doctors ordered one of his brain. Knowing what I know now, I can hardly believe I wrote at that time, "We don't think there is a reason to be concerned; they are just very thorough." All the medical personnel knew there was much reason to be concerned, but they graciously never told us what they expected. And with child-like faith, I simply continued to believe that Christian would make a full recovery.

My song for that day, sent by a friend, was one I'd never heard before, but it was spot-on. "Calling for a Flood," by John Waller, includes these words:

> Flood every corner of this room.
> Flood all the emptiness with You.
> Lord, I long to be consumed
> And I'm calling for a flood.

> SO FLOOD EVERY CHAMBER OF MY HEART.
> Flood what I lack with what You are.
> I am dry and I am parched
> And I'm calling for a flood.

The lyrics that I capitalized seemed particularly significant for someone recovering from a cardiac arrest.

In the wee hours the next morning, the nurses gave Christian an opportunity to breathe on his own… and he rocked it! That was a huge step toward Christian getting his breathing tube out. But frustratingly, he couldn't have it removed now until after the MRI of his brain, which was scheduled for late that evening.

Up until this point, John had been home and to his job a couple of times, but I had no intentions of leaving the hospital. Early that morning, it dawned on me that it made sense for me to drive home that day and let John stay with Christian. John's bosses had been wonderful about allowing him to work from the hospital, and that day his phone and laptop enabled him to do all that he needed to do. The doctors planned to keep Christian in his coma all day and the MRI wasn't happening until after 6 p.m. I needed to pay our monthly bills and my hairdresser graciously allowed me to un-cancel the appointment I'd already canceled. From the time I first got the idea to drive home until I left the hospital, only about 30 minutes elapsed. I'm glad I didn't have much time to think about what lay in store.

For as long as I can remember, driving in cities has scared me to death. I could probably count on one hand the number of times I'd ever done it.

Growing up in a rural area, I'd never had any reason to drive in the city, so I never learned the skill. But I determined that if God could part the Red Sea to let the Israelites cross on dry land, he could part the traffic on Route 28 for me. The day Christian collapsed (and every time I've been there since), traffic on Route 28 was three lanes, bumper-to-bumper, moving at high speeds. John had warned me that when heading home, I would have about one-half mile to work my way across all three lanes of that terrifying traffic to get to the exit I needed. But on that glorious morning, when I came down the entrance ramp onto Route 28, there was not one single car in sight in any of the three oncoming lanes. Oh, thank you, sweet Jesus!

On my return trip, at the last red light before merging onto the dreaded Route 28, the license plate on the vehicle in front of me said, "PRAYZ1," which gave me great peace. I returned safely to the hospital with the bills paid, a new haircut, and a sense of accomplishment.

During the quiet times, John and I drew encouragement and strength from hundreds of personal emails and Facebook messages. We appreciated every single one, but those that provided the most comfort were those in which the specific prayers for us were written out. I know it's much faster to post the word "praying" or an emoji of praying hands, and we truly welcomed every such message, but I now try (not always successfully) to take the time to type out my prayers to those going through hard times. I also cherished the posts that spoke prophetically about Christian's future.

The messages that completely wrecked me, though, were the ones I didn't see coming. That afternoon, I was reading a newsletter from the school board at Portersville Christian School, trying to keep up with all the things we were missing. The last paragraph caught me completely off guard. It said:

> We also ask a special prayer request for the Cater family. Please lift their family and especially Christian in prayer during this time. The power of prayer is a wondrous force to behold. The power of prayer should never be underestimated because it draws on the

glory and might of the infinitely powerful God. James 5:16-18 declares, "The prayer of a righteous man is powerful and effective."

Amen to that!

I had a similar experience the week before in reading a routine email from Christian's basketball coach to the entire team. Basketball practices began, without Christian, two days after soccer season ended. The coach was simply giving basic instructions about practices, but it was what he wrote after his signature that took my breath away... #prayingforChristian. For the next several months, he ended all of his basketball emails that way and he turned out to be one of Christian's biggest cheerleaders.

In fact, when I got back to the hospital that day, I was greeted by four 20 by 30 inch foam posters that the basketball coach had initiated. Each one featured a large cutout picture of Christian playing either soccer or basketball, and they were signed by both elementary and high school students from his school. Together, the four stretched the full length of the sofa in Christian's room.

Throughout the time that Christian was in the induced coma, I wondered frequently what he was experiencing. Was he playing soccer with Jesus? Hanging out with the angels? Could he hear our words to him and the praise music playing in his ear?

Two comments we received about his coma stood out to me. Someone who didn't even know us wrote:

"Absent from the body; present before the Lord."

A friend compared his being in a coma with a butterfly in a chrysalis.

"In the chrysalis stage, God is protecting you, holding you close to his heart till you fully recover, and then beyond, to soar above circumstance."

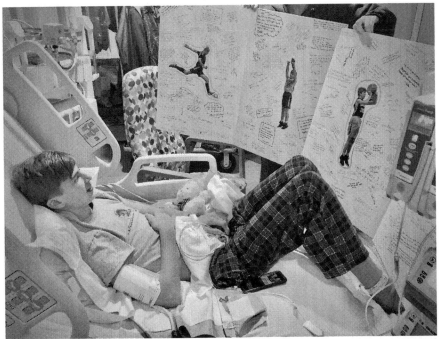

Christian looks at the posters from his basketball coach, which were signed by many of the students at his school.

That afternoon, we had to give up our peaceful room at the end of the hallway. Evidently, it contained some special equipment that was needed for an incoming patient, so we were relocated to a room directly across from the sole door into the PICU, as well as the main medical station on the floor. Because of the constant activity, the second room was much noisier than the first.

That night, Christian got an MRI of his brain, and the results were normal. Since I had been expecting complete healing ever since he was anointed, I had no idea how miraculous that was. Finishing the last MRI set the stage for his breathing tube to come out the next day.

I woke up the next morning, November 2, so excited for Christian to get the breathing tube removed so he could talk to us. The doctors kindly explained to John and me that we would not want to be in the room while they were taking it out because we might see and hear things that would make us squeamish. We readily agreed to wait in a lounge area near Christian's room.

The procedure was supposed to be fairly short, but time was dragging on longer than we'd been told to expect. We didn't know enough about the situation to suspect something was wrong, but in the end, Christian's pneumonia was worse than the doctors had realized, and he was not yet ready to be off the darn breathing tube. I was so disappointed that he was put back into the induced coma to heal some more. In hindsight, John and I calculate that the pneumonia added a full week to Christian's recovery and overrode the doctor's prediction that he'd be released in two weeks.

Fortunately, we got lots of company that day, so I didn't have time to dwell on the setback. And, unbeknownst to us at the time, one of our visitors came bearing information that would change the course of Christian's treatment.

CHAPTER 4

W e knew that the husband of one of our close friends worked in the medical field, but we'd never really understood what he did. It turned out he worked for the company that made the type of defibrillator the doctors intended to implant in Christian, and his job was to sit in on surgeries and make sure the devices were implanted correctly. He gave us a list of the pros and cons of that type of traditional defibrillator as well as a different style known as an S-ICD, which stands for subcutaneous implantable cardioverter defibrillator.

At that time, John and I saw that both types of defibrillators had quite a few drawbacks, and we still hoped a way might be found for Christian to avoid getting one at all. As long as we focused on Christian's day-to-day care, it was easy to put off deciding about the defibrillators, and we put that very important information on a back burner.

It was much nicer to focus on our company. A niece who we don't get to see very often drove five hours to spend time with us. Two of Christian's closest friends from church came to the hospital, too. They were the first teen guests he had had, and they desperately wanted to see him. John and I had been briefing adult visitors on how many tubes and machines Christian was hooked to and then giving them the choice of whether they wanted to see him or visit with us in a waiting room. Some chose each way. But we felt strongly that, even though the kids' hearts were in the right place, we needed to protect them from being traumatized by seeing Christian in the condition he was in. So, John and I agreed not to allow any teens to see him until after the medical gadgetry was gone.

Even though I was extremely disappointed that the breathing tube wasn't removed that day, I continued to hang on to my song du jour, which was

"Lord You Have my Heart" by Delirious. I hadn't heard it until a friend sent us the fitting lyrics:

> Lord, You have my heart, and I will search for Yours
> Jesus, take my life and lead me on
> Oh, Lord, You have my heart, and I will search for Yours
> Let me be to You a sacrifice, and I will praise You, Lord
> And I will sing of love come down
> And as You show Your face, we'll see Your glory here.

Meanwhile, for several days, John had had the line running through his head, "It's Friday... but Sunday's comin'." That originally referred to the darkness and sadness of Good Friday vs. the glorious joy of Easter Sunday in a sermon by S.M. Lockridge. It particularly struck us now, because the day that the doctors were unable to remove the breathing tube was a Friday... and they planned to try again on Sunday. So, we clung to the phrase, "But Sunday's comin'."

While we waited, I received an encouraging text from an old friend we'd recently reconnected with when she ordered subs from Christian for the youth group's fundraiser. She described her drive home from work and said that as she was praying for Christian, she spotted a rainbow from out of nowhere... and it hadn't even been raining that day! She included a photo of the rainbow that she was able to take with her cell phone, and said that since the day Christian collapsed, she had been thanking God for his healing.

Saturday evening, John and I enjoyed a brief respite from the hospital world. A friend used Facetime on her cell phone to enable us to watch Christian's soccer banquet while he slept through it. As a freshman, it would have been his first one, and I was so disappointed that he had to miss it, especially when he earned his first athletic letter. Soccer had been his passion since he was five and, while I was excited and proud that he'd received a letter, I so wished he could've been there to receive the reward for all his hard work.

When Sunday finally arrived, I shared this summary with our prayer warriors on Facebook:

We had our best day yet yesterday, followed by our roughest night. Both were likely because Christian is only lightly sedated now, and therefore able to communicate with us. It is wonderful that he can answer yes or no questions to tell us if something is uncomfortable, when he needs his lungs suctioned, whether he is cold, etc. This has empowered him to have some control over his own care.

Without going into details that would embarrass him, let's just say his pride remains strong and his feistiness never waivers. And these are GOOD things usually... except in the middle of the night, when there are many interruptions to his sleep, and he gets agitated. Every time we got him calmed down last night, another medical person needed him to do something, and the hullabaloo started all over again. I think we got about two hours' sleep.

Frustratingly, the prayer focus remains on clearing the pneumonia from his lungs. He was a champ at doing what he could to clear his lungs Saturday, but more gunk forms as fast as he expels it. We were hoping today would be the big day when the breathing tube came out, but the doctor said he is still not ready.

We are disappointed again but standing on Psalm 34:1-5, "I bless God every chance I get; my lungs expand with his praise. I live and breathe God; if things aren't going well, hear this and be happy: join me in spreading the news; together let's get the word out. God met me more than halfway. He freed me from my anxious fears. Look at him; give him your warmest smile. Never hide your feelings from him." Today's song is "The Solid Rock" (by William B. Bradbury), which includes these words:

*My hope is built on nothing less
Than Jesus' blood and righteousness;
I dare not trust the sweetest frame
But wholly lean on Jesus' name.*

*On Christ, the solid Rock, I stand
All other ground is sinking sand.
All other ground is sinking sand.*

*When darkness veils His lovely face,
I rest on His unchanging grace.
In every high and stormy gale,
My anchor holds within the veil.*

*His oath, His covenant, His blood,
Support me in the whelming flood;
When all around my soul gives way,
He then is all my hope and stay.*

Despite our high hopes based on "It's Friday... but Sunday's comin,'" doctors said Christian's pneumonia was still "pretty significant" so they couldn't try to remove his breathing tube yet. And the maddening wait went on.

The next few days of Christian's hospital stay were our most demanding and exhausting. Christian was experiencing delirium, which a handout from the hospital explained as "a change in a person's thinking or behavior caused by changes in how the brain is working." The handout listed several possible symptoms, and the ones that hit Christian the hardest were inconsolableness that wouldn't respond to usual soothing; behavior or emotions that are different than usual, including aggression and suspicion; seeing or hearing things that aren't real but seem very real; agitation, restless movements, pulling out lines or other important medical devices.

Even though Christian lost 23 pounds from his already slender frame, and even though his hands were tied down to prevent him from pulling out his breathing tube or any needles, John and I had to restrain him multiple times daily. Because of the delirium, he would frequently thrash wildly. Most of the time, John and I could hold him down ourselves, but sometimes it took six people to keep him from hurting himself.

We had been warned that if Christian pulled out his breathing tube that he could do permanent damage to his vocal cords, so we were highly motivated to keep him as calm as possible. But the delirium made Christian do things he'd never do normally, and his fear gave him unnatural strength. At one point, Christian put his foot on my breastbone and pushed. He threw me off balance and only by the grace of God did I avoid knocking over the metal pole containing his many medications.

During one of those evenings, Christian was assigned a nurse whose honesty I will always appreciate. Up until this time, every hospital employee who had had contact with Christian was phenomenal in their abilities. But as the day nurse was instructing the nurse coming on duty, I sensed that she was not qualified to take care of someone in Christian's condition. I had already informed John quietly that he and I were going to have to take turns staying up all night because I didn't feel comfortable with the new nurse. Before bedtime, Christian went into one of his wild fits. Even as several people battled to hold him still, I observed that our nurse was shying away from Christian.

Shortly after the crisis had passed, the nurse came to John and me, apologizing. She recognized that she was in over her head with Christian and had requested to change assignments with a more experienced nurse. She further confided that she had been struggling with some personal issues that perhaps were clouding her mind. I was nothing but relieved that she had excused herself from Christian's care! The more she apologized, the more we thanked and praised her for putting Christian's needs above her pride. John and I were able to pray with her before she moved on to her new assignment, and we gratefully embraced the new nurse, who was more than capable of dealing with Christian.

After a few days and nights of minimal sleep and frequent physical battles, John and I were beyond exhausted and emotionally drained. At one of my lowest points, I had an amazing experience with the power of praising God. John was sleeping, and I desperately wanted to be, but Christian couldn't be left alone. Through tears, I forced myself to sing along with the praise music that played almost continually in Christian's room. Midway through the second song, I told God I was so weak that I needed his strength. I don't even remember what song was playing, but the very next line that played was about God being our strength. My circumstances had not changed at all, but the power of praise renewed me and gave me strength for the battle.

Dealing with the delirium was by far the hardest part of Christian's recovery. While my body was so drained, my mind started having a pity party. Christian's birthday was only two days away, and I finally accepted that he wasn't going to be able to enjoy any type of normal celebration. I hated that Christian had to go through any of this to begin with, but missing his own birthday celebration just seemed too cruel. But I suddenly realized how thankful I was that Christian was even alive for his 15th birthday. I acknowledged that he would have many more birthdays to celebrate in the future and that it wasn't the end of the world to miss one. That was the point at which I realized the power of perspective. Absolutely nothing had changed, but the way I looked at the situation made all the difference.

At lunchtime on November 5, Day 13 of our hospital stay, John put out an SOS on Facebook that said:

> Christian has been in a lot of pain for the past 12 hours. His abdomen is causing him great pain, and he has just started getting leg cramps. He is also very itchy. He is flat-out miserable. Please pray for relief from all the symptoms and for the doctors to figure out how to help him. He hasn't slept all night.

Within 36 minutes of posting that plea, Christian began to improve dramatically. He was finally able to get some much-needed rest, and doctors determined the cause of his stomach pain had to do with him not eating for so long and some of the medicine he'd been on.

During that brief respite, John and I finally came up with an idea for all the kind people who had been offering to help us with anything we needed. We realized it was the time of year that Christian usually selected items to pack in a shoebox for a ministry called Samaritan's Purse to distribute to destitute children all around the world. Since Christian couldn't participate this year, we invited his Facebook prayer warriors to fill boxes on his behalf.

And, boy, did they respond! More than 50 boxes were donated in honor of Christian. In a normal year, Christian and I pack two boxes, so I just loved how the Lord multiplied our meager offering. This reminded me so much of a story in the Bible where Jesus took one young boy's lunch, multiplied it, and used it to feed 5,000 men, plus women and children. We didn't reach 5,000 boxes, but I was delighted that, even in Christian's condition, God still could use him to accomplish good in this world.

We hope that Christian's experience also helped accomplish some good in the medical community. We were invited to participate in a research study and readily allowed Christian's information to be used to benefit someone else's child going through a similar situation in the future. The study focused on children whose hearts had stopped or who had needed CPR. The goal of the study, *Personalizing Outcomes After Child Cardiac Arrest* (POCCA), was learning to predict long-term outcomes, especially on the brain, based on Christian's progress. (Months later, when we were contacted for a follow-up, I told the researcher I wasn't sure Christian's results would be much help because he'd been miraculously healed.)

Our fitting song of the day was "Oceans" by Hillsong United. The lyrics include:

You call me out upon the waters
The great unknown where feet may fail
And there I find You in the mystery
In oceans deep
My faith will stand

And I will call upon Your name
And keep my eyes above the waves

When oceans rise, my soul will rest in Your embrace
For I am Yours and You are mine.

Your grace abounds in deepest waters
Your sovereign hand
Will be my guide
Where feet may fail and fear surrounds me
You've never failed and You won't start now

Spirit lead me where my trust is without borders
Let me walk upon the waters
Wherever You would call me
Take me deeper than my feet could ever wander
And my faith will be made stronger
In the presence of my Savior.

The next day, things started looking up, largely because the doctors removed a buildup of mucus from Christian's lungs. One of them even proclaimed that Christian's "airway looked pristine." I'm not sure why they didn't remove the plug sooner, but once it was gone, the way was cleared to remove that darned breathing tube and plans were to try, once again, to take it out the next day, Christian's birthday.

Christian's brain was working clearly this day. He recognized people, did some elementary problem-solving, and even minded his manners by mouthing the words "thank you."

He was doing so well that John and I slipped away for a while. John's cousin and her daughter, who was off duty as a nurse in the hospital's Neonatal Intensive Care Unit, stayed with Christian while John and I went to vote. In the midst of everything going on at the hospital, I had managed to call our county's voter registration office the week before to request absentee ballots. Much to my frustration, I was informed that the deadline had passed to request them. I was pretty snarky when I "apologized" for not scheduling my son's cardiac arrest at a more convenient time. We had been disappointed, thinking that we weren't going to be able to vote, but everything worked out to enable us to do it in person.

That day, we received a get-well card that contained a Bible verse that was incredibly fitting. Psalm 73:26 says, "My flesh and my heart may fail, but God is the strength of my heart and my portion forever."

Our song *du jour* was "Whom Shall I Fear" by Chris Tomlin. It contains these lyrics:

You hear me when I call. You are my morning song.
Though darkness fills the night, it cannot hide the light.
Whom shall I fear?

You crush the enemy underneath my feet
You are my sword and shield
Though troubles linger still,
Whom shall I fear?

I know who goes before me
I know who stands behind.
The God of angel armies is always by my side.

My strength is in Your name, for You alone can save
You will deliver me; Yours is the victory
Whom shall I fear? Whom shall I fear?

And nothing formed against me shall stand
You hold the whole world in Your hands
I'm holding on to Your promises
You are faithful; You are faithful.

We truly did not know what to expect the next day when the breathing tube came out. We had been warned that Christian might have the world's worst sore throat from having the tube in. Nevertheless, we all went to bed that night with high hopes for the next day... but we never could've anticipated how it all would play out.

CHAPTER 5

When the team of doctors visited Christian the next morning, all systems were go for the best birthday present we could think of: getting rid of his breathing tube. The plan was for the doctors to take it out after they finished making their rounds, probably in the late morning. But Mr. Impatient Pants couldn't wait that long. Around 8:45 a.m., a routine check uncovered an urgent problem with Christian's breathing tube that necessitated immediate attention. I was under the impression that he had pulled it out. I was bewildered that it had stayed in through days' worth of delirium and thrashing but come out while he was lying calmly. More importantly, I remembered the warning that if he pulled it out himself, he could do permanent damage to his vocal cords.

Within seconds, 12 medical staffers filled our room, trapping John and me inside. Now, I remembered clearly from a previous attempt to remove the tube that the doctors had cautioned us we wouldn't want to be in the room when it came out because we would see and hear things we'd probably prefer not to experience. I had no desire to be in the room, but I couldn't get out. So, I closed my eyes, plugged my ears, and prayed intensely. I took my fingers out of my ears long enough to shoot out an emergency message, "Christian needs prayer NOW!" then went back into my own little world.

After the crisis passed, one of Christian's doctors came over to check on me. I imagine I looked pretty odd, but I managed to block out all sights and sounds, so I was fine. I so completely snuffed out all noises that I went through the entire day thinking that Christian had pulled out his breathing tube. It wasn't until 12 hours later that John explained to me that it had only come loose, rather than out.

At long last, we were free from the breathing tube, but the emergency removal had a very challenging side effect: nurses hadn't had a chance to wean Christian off some of his medications, so he likely was experiencing some withdrawal along with the delirium. He was wild.

While well-wishes for his birthday poured in, John and I waged our toughest battle yet. I'm not sure why, but that day, no hospital employees helped us hold him down. It was brutal. At one point, I shot a text to one of Christian's cousins, who'd planned to visit him for his birthday, and just said, "Not a good day. Please don't come."

The best news was that Christian was able to whisper. I was thankful that, even if he had damaged his vocal cords, he still could communicate that much. Mercifully, he never experienced a sore throat from the ordeal with the breathing tube. Christian also was able to request water, which he was allowed to suck out of a wet washcloth.

Physically, it was a good day. Besides the breathing tube, doctors also were able to remove Christian's feeding tube and some other tubes and needles. His digestive system started working with minimal pain and his pneumonia continued to improve.

Even so, Christian was such a train wreck emotionally that we chose not to even mention to him that it was his birthday.

As John described it that night, "It was the best of times, it was the worst of times. It was a Dickens of a day."

Late in the day, when John and I were about at the end of our ropes, a professional from Supportive Care visited us for the first time. We called her our angel. She recommended some changes to his medications to reduce his agitation but, most importantly, she arranged for some helpers to sit with Christian, so we weren't holding him down by ourselves.

The Supportive Care doctor told us that one of the best ways to overcome delirium was to find ways to reorient the patient. She recommended we try to keep him awake during the day and sleep at night; that we let him see people he'd like to see; and that we bring pictures, blankets, and other things from home that were familiar and safe.

John jumped right on the last recommendation. Without my knowledge, he contacted one of our friends and asked her to drive to our house, gather some items from Christian's bedroom, and drive them to us that night. And she is such a sweetheart, she did it! I was incredulous when I found out he'd asked her to drive to the hospital so late at night. In my opinion, the request easily could have waited until morning. I keep telling John that someday I will forgive him for that. But I know he was just doing all he could to alleviate the chaos in Christian's mind.

The song we hung on to that day was "Blessed Be Your Name," by Matt Redman:

> Blessed be Your name
> In the land that is plentiful
> Where Your streams of abundance flow
> Blessed be Your name
>
> Blessed be Your name
> When I'm found in the desert place
> Though I walk through the wilderness
> Blessed be Your name
>
> Every blessing You pour out, I'll
> Turn back to praise
> When the darkness closes in, Lord
> Still, I will say
>
> Blessed be the name of the Lord
> Blessed be Your name
> Blessed be the name of the Lord
> Blessed be Your glorious name
>
> Blessed be Your name
> When the sun's shining down on me
> When the world's all as it should be
> Blessed be Your name

Blessed be Your name
On the road marked with suffering
Though there's pain in the offering
Blessed be Your name

You give and take away
You give and take away
My heart will choose to say,
Lord, blessed be Your name

It certainly wasn't the birthday celebration we'd have hoped for, but our boy was alive, and after 15 days, his breathing tube was history.

On Day 16, Christian finally turned the corner and never looked back. He progressed by leaps and bounds on all fronts. He was able to talk with us, albeit very softly. He was allowed to eat for the first time since his cardiac arrest. He sat up in a chair for an hour. And the twinkle was back in his eyes.

Three conversations that day reassured me that Christian's memory was functioning fairly well. His nurse's name that day was Jena (pronounced Jenna). When he learned her name, it reminded him of a girl with the same name who had been in his class in kindergarten and first grade. He asked if it was the same Jena. I told him no, but that I happened to know that the other Jenna and two additional classmates had been praying for him. I asked if he remembered the three girls and he looked at me like I had three heads. "Of course I do," he emphasized, as if to imply, "Why wouldn't I?"

Later on, Christian was wheedling nurse Jena for more water. He was scheduled for a swallow test and wasn't supposed to be drinking anything. He asked and asked and asked, and Jena held firm. In thirsty desperation, Christian tried a new tack and asked for "agua," which is Spanish for water. She caved. We soon texted Christian's Spanish teacher and asked if he could earn some extra credit for using one of his vocabulary words. She said yes.

Those two incidents showed me that he had at least some long-term and short-term memory functions.

The third telling conversation requires a little background. Christian likes to receive balloons for his birthday, and he'd been nervously keeping an eye on the situation at the local dollar store where I normally buy his birthday balloons. They had been experiencing shortages of helium for several weeks and had been unable to sell balloons. He had researched the situation and discovered that we were experiencing a worldwide helium shortage.

So, this day, he lay in his bed, carefully, somberly studying the many varied balloons adorning his room. He reached up and grabbed my collar and pulled me down to him, so I could hear him say softly, "Do you remember I told you there's a worldwide helium shortage?" Of all the things he could fixate on after two weeks in oblivion, he chose to focus on helium. Go figure!

The entire time that Christian was in a coma, I was just itching to find out what he was experiencing in the spiritual realm. I was hoping for grand stories of heaven, Jesus, and angels, but the reality was much less exciting.

At one point, out of the blue, Christian pointed to the ceiling and said, "I should be up there." John and I assured him that he was exactly where God wanted him to be. Later, he talked about crossing a river with Jesus and seeing "Poppy" on the bank on the other side. We assume he was referring to my deceased father, whom Christian had called PopPop. When we asked Christian who else was on the shore, he said, "Lots of people." But that was all he ever said about the time while he was unconscious, and now he doesn't even remember saying those things. So, all the information I'd hoped to hear about remains a mystery.

Once Christian was conscious, lucid, and able to communicate, medical personnel came out of the woodwork. In addition to the myriad doctors and nurses caring for him, he now added speech therapists, physical therapists, occupational therapists, rehabilitative services, child life specialists, and probably several more. There was such a steady stream of people coming to work with him that we had to start asking some to come back later, just so the boy could eat his meals.

Much to Christian's frustration, many of the specialists asked the same questions. He just wanted to get on with life, and several of the folks kept asking him to spell "world" backward and similar neurological tests. I wasn't too concerned that he couldn't do it because, in my sleep-deprived state, I couldn't either!

They also kept asking him where he was and for a couple of days, he kept saying "Butler Hospital." We tried to explain to the therapists that there was some validity for him to say that. I had been a patient in Butler Memorial Hospital just a couple of weeks before he collapsed, and shortly before that, we had visited his beloved music teacher when she was a patient there. And he wasn't conscious when he was transported to Children's Hospital, so it made sense that the last hospital he remembered being in was Butler. Still, we had to correct him several times before he was able to provide the right answer to the question.

By far, my favorite question from a therapist was when one pointed to me and asked, "Who's that?"

Christian responded, "Mom. I could never forget Mom." I melted. At that moment, the boy could have asked me for a-n-y-t-h-i-n-g and I would've given it to him on a silver platter.

During this time, Christian was still getting periodic breathing treatments, which he loathed. He struggled so much with the first one that they had to cut it short. At that time, I challenged him to come up with a way to get through the next one. When the staff came for the second breathing treatment, I asked Christian if he'd thought of a coping mechanism. He replied, "Holy Ghost." He had remembered! Throughout the first half of the treatment, he kept repeating those two words. He needed to take a short break to regroup and for the second portion, he sang/hummed "I've got peace like a river..." And he conquered the test! I was so very, very proud of him.

For the first time in five days, I finally had time to write in my little red journal again. That entry, directed toward Christian, said:

> If you learn nothing else from this hospital stay, I believe you are learning how to make your faith your own, and hang on to Jesus during the times you have no other option. You are seeing there are things in life that Mommy and Daddy *can't* do with/for you. Only Jesus can walk through these situations with you. Learn this lesson well, my son; it will serve you well throughout your life.

That evening, Christian was up for a short wheelchair ride around the PICU. We hadn't expected the extent of communication among staff on the floor. We still hadn't told him he'd missed celebrating his birthday, but so many friendly nurses mentioned his birthday to him, that we had to fess up. To soften the news, we told him about the giant birthday party I'd promised him if he got better. He took it all in stride and got busy making plans for what he wanted at his party.

Another sign that our guy was returning to normal was the reemergence of his sense of humor. As Christian chattered happily about what drinks he wanted for his big party, the dear soul who was sitting with him that night to relieve John and me asked him what foods he wanted for it.

Without missing a beat, Christian said to her with a mischievous grin, "Whatever you bring!"

By this time, Christian's wild thrashing was winding down, but the delirium still was affecting his mind. He insisted that one of the kind women who came to sit with him was a thief. There was also a jovial gentleman who had many fun stories and reminded John and me a lot of one of Christian's dear uncles. But the suspicion that can accompany delirium was still running high, and Christian must have called him "sketchy" 30 times, thankfully, never when the man could hear.

Oddly enough, for the first time since Christian's collapse, I did not receive a song to sustain me through the day. Perhaps that was because I didn't need it as desperately since I could plainly see Christian's progress.

CHAPTER 6

B y the next day, Christian was improving so rapidly that I began to entertain notions of taking him home. Since we'd had to spend his birthday in the hospital, my focus shifted to getting him home in time for Thanksgiving, which is Christian's favorite holiday. But then I learned that hospital policy does not allow anyone to get discharged directly from the PICU; all the children have to spend some time on a regular floor for continued care and observation.

Later that day, John and I were asked to consider sending Christian to inpatient rehabilitation after he was discharged from the hospital. In my eyes, he was returning to normal just fine, but my dreams of getting him home for Thanksgiving were slipping further away.

Even though Christian had passed a swallow test the day before and was happily eating and drinking all he could, one of the therapists spotted something that concerned her. She ordered a more extensive type of swallow test, dubbed a cookie test, which unfortunately showed Christian wasn't safe to have anything liquid because he was at high risk for silent aspiration. According to Google, aspiration describes a condition when food or fluids that should go into the stomach go into the lungs instead. Usually, when this happens, the person coughs to clear the item from their lungs. However, sometimes the person doesn't cough at all, which is known as silent aspiration.

Christian wasn't allowed to have any ice cream, soup, popsicles, or Jell-O. But, worst of all, he also couldn't drink any liquids that weren't thickened with a packet of Honey Thick. The thickener distorted the taste of all beverages and this restriction, to Christian, was far and away the worst part of his entire ordeal.

Despite the problems swallowing, Christian was progressing so well that medical personnel decided he was ready to move from the PICU to a regular room. While preparations were being made for the move, Christian received a very special visitor.

One of the cardiac doctors who had worked on Christian the day he was admitted sought him out, just to shake his hand. After he chatted amicably with Christian for a short while, he motioned for me to follow him into the hall, out of Christian's earshot.

"That boy's a miracle," he said flat out.

I asked why he said that, and he said that based on the EKGs provided by the emergency medical technicians who responded to our house and how long Christian's brain was without oxygen, he "expected a very different outcome."

I asked if that meant he hadn't believed Christian would survive. He said that once doctors got Christian stabilized, he expected him to live. But he expected "significant brain damage."

That was the first time I'd heard Christian described as a miracle, and it was also the first time I got a hint of what the doctors had known all along about the extent of Christian's brain damage. His words gave me much to contemplate.

We were just an ordinary family, but perhaps the Lord was using us to showcase His extraordinary power.

As we neared the time to move to a regular hospital room, one of the nurses who had worked most closely with Christian pulled me aside. She also described Christian as a miracle. Again, I asked why she said that, and she said simply, "Because I saw his EKGs." She went on to say that she'd worked in the PICU for seven years. "I see miracles in here all the time," she said. "But he's in the top three."

As important as those words were, I didn't have much time to digest them before we were whisked off to Christian's new room on a different floor, where we made an accidentally grand arrival. The new room had much less storage space than the previous one, and as John and I busied ourselves settling in, we heard some pretty bells or chimes sounding.

Soon, several nurses and aides appeared in our room, and I thought how nice it was that they'd all come to welcome us. As it turned out, the pleasant bells were sounding an SOS that there was an emergency in our room. But nobody could figure out why they were chiming. The entire wing we were staying in had been remodeled and reopened a couple of days earlier, so even the nurses weren't familiar with some of the features yet. One of them finally realized that when I'd hung my jacket on a hook in the bathroom, it pressed an alarm button.

Oh well, sometimes we needed a little levity in our lives! For example, John came up with a game that we played every time we used the elevators. Each floor had four elevators grouped together, and we each went and stood beside the one we guessed would arrive first. We kept a running tally of which of us selected the proper one. By the time Christian was discharged, John was ahead by two or three.

I also realized how unobservant I am when it comes to reading signs. One day, when Christian had been in the PICU for about two weeks, I spotted a sign right beside the only door into the unit. It said that food and drinks were prohibited in the PICU. Now, not only did we have a small pantry set up in our room by that time, but I'd joked with the receptionists on multiple occasions about some of the goodies that friends and family were supplying to us. And not one of them ever tried to stop me. I truly am a rule-follower, and I *never* would've disobeyed the sign... if I'd seen it. But in the ignorance-is-bliss category, it sure was convenient to have so many of our meals at our fingertips, so we didn't have to leave Christian.

Christian continued to thrive in his new room. He was sent for another MRI, which was ever-so-much simpler than the lengthy preparation required when he was covered by machines from head to toe. We were overjoyed to learn that the results showed no damage to Christian's heart.

He was encouraged to sit up or even take short walks as much as possible. By then, the pneumonia was pretty much gone, and the more he moved around, the less likely it was to return. He was feeling so much better that he was getting bored. We all agreed that he was ready for some visits from his peers.

O ur first gathering included a niece, a good friend, and her teenage son, who had grown up with Christian. All six of us had served together on a mission trip a couple of years earlier, so it was a nice mini reunion. Our niece presented Christian with a soft handmade Penn State blanket. It was quite a conversation-starter with medical personnel, and we quickly determined which ones were Penn State fans and which ones preferred the University of Pittsburgh. The visit boosted Christian's spirits, and we happily set about scheduling more.

The first time Christian is up to having visitors. From left: His cousin Amy McKoy, and friends Zach and Lisa Labon.

The next day, a family we know from Christian's school came to see us and brought supper, along with a very clear example of God's loving attention to the little things. The family had no idea that every year Christian chose a giant chocolate chip cookie instead of a birthday cake. John and I had had no opportunity to buy him the jumbo cookie, but on a whim, they picked one up for him. It touched my heart that God cared about even those little details for Christian.

During that period, Christian started making good use of the cell phone he'd received as an early birthday present. I can't recall ever giving him an early birthday present before, but we'd given him the cell phone so he would have it for the soccer tournament that he never got to attend. In God's divine providence, Christian already had his friends' numbers in the phone, and it was ready to go.

His first attempts at texting were complete gibberish, as his mind and hands weren't working together yet, and he gave some of his friends a major challenge in trying to respond to his unintelligible posts. But by now, he was able to communicate much better, and he reveled at being able to stay in touch with his friends.

My Facebook post for November 13, which was Day 21 of our hospital stay, read:

> Christian continues to strengthen physically and improve cognitively each day. John and I need your prayers right now as we make decisions about his future therapy and treatment. There are no clear-cut, easy answers and I feel like I am being given a final exam in a foreign language (medical) that I've only been learning for a few days.
>
> For the first time, Christian is able to contribute to this update. He asked that I tell you all, "Thanks for praying."
>
> Christian now knows pretty much everything we do about what happened to him and has a general idea of what needs to happen before he can come home. That was a lot for him to swallow in

one day. He seems to be handling it decently and is determined to do whatever it takes to get home ASAP. The cardiac doctor recognizes this situation can be overwhelming for a young man who has never been sick, and he encouraged us to consider finding a psychiatrist or psychologist who has worked with kids who have gone through similar experiences. (*Note: Nearly four years after the cardiac arrest, Christian continues to insist he doesn't need counseling and declines our offers.*) We ask for your prayers to help Christian process this mind-boggling situation.

Christian very much seemed to connect with a newspaper story about a colonel who was in the Pentagon on 9/11. Col. Douglas Lengenfelder said, "When you fight on the side of angels, you fight with the strength of thousands. When you fight for yourself, you fight by yourself." He went on to say that if he had died when the Pentagon was struck, "It would have been OK. That would have been my time. But it wasn't. It wasn't me because God has more for me to do before it's my turn."

Please do not worry if you do not hear from us daily. Yesterday was so crazy busy that I actually had to politely ask one very important doctor to please come back later. After Christian had seen four doctors and therapists in a row, the poor kid needed to go to the bathroom and, even though it was nearly lunchtime, he hadn't gotten to eat his breakfast yet. Even his nurses have to wait in line to give him his medications...

For the past few days, I have been able to do morning devotions, and I had thought perhaps that was why God had stopped sending me songs. When I got up this morning, I was apprehensive because John went to work today, and I am anticipating some complicated medical discussions. But God dropped an old chorus ("This Is the Day" by Joe Pace) into my heart, which is carrying me:

This is the day, this is the day
That the Lord has made, that the Lord has made.
We will rejoice, we will rejoice
And be glad in it, and be glad in it.
This is the day that the Lord has made,
We will rejoice and be glad in it,
This is the day, this is the day,
That the Lord has made.

My son is *alive...* I do not have to wait until he is home to be grateful and enjoy the day.

M y apprehension about that day proved to be correct, as I encountered the only doctor during our entire hospital stay who completely rubbed me the wrong way. I hesitate to even mention this, but it allows me to emphasize how fantastic the other doctors and nurses all were.

Ever since Christian's breathing tube came out, he spoke more softly than normal. An ear, nose, and throat (ENT) doctor was summoned to do a quick but very unpleasant procedure to see inside Christian's vocal cords. Christian had a Child Life Specialist whose job included walking him through any procedures or surgeries he faced. She had told us to page her as soon as the ENT doctor arrived, so she could help Christian through the process.

Although I explained to the ENT doctor that the woman was on her way, he forged right ahead with the nasty prep. Thank goodness the Child Life Specialist arrived quickly because he had no intention of waiting for her. With a little patience and explanation, that procedure wouldn't have been nearly as obnoxious as it was. Christian barely ate or drank anything for the rest of the day, which wasn't good for a young man trying to regain the 23 pounds he lost while in the induced coma.

Unfortunately, the procedure did prove important. Through it, we learned that Christian's right vocal cord was not moving. We had been warned that if he pulled out his breathing tube, he could permanently damage his vocal cords. Evidently, when it got dislodged on its own, it still did some damage. The ENT doctor was not encouraging about the future. He said the vocal cord might or might not begin working again, but that it would take weeks or months for that to occur. Further, he said that no medical treatment existed to get it moving. As a last resort, he said the vocal cord could be injected, in a procedure requiring anesthesia, which would help it work for about three months. But no permanent solutions existed.

Instead, we relied on the speech therapists, who started giving him voice exercises to get the vocal cord moving again, and, most importantly, our faithful prayer warriors, who immediately began interceding that the vocal cord would start working again.

After the ENT trauma, our day took a giant turn for the better when a crew from a local radio station asked to interview Christian and me. KDKA, the station I always listen to for news, does an annual Christmas-time fund drive for Children's Hospital and they were looking for sound bites to promote it.

A few weeks later, when my morning alarm went off, I heard a story that sounded very similar to our own. I didn't recognize my own voice, and in my groggy state, it took me a minute to realize it *was* me. That was the only time I heard the promo on the air, and Christian never did hear it, but it was nice to be able to support the hospital that had done so much for us.

When John returned to the hospital the next morning, he came with exciting news that gave us hope that Christian wouldn't need a defibrillator implanted after all. Our brother-in-law remembered that a couple of years earlier, John had collapsed in the same bathroom that Christian did. He'd done a little research and wondered if possibly faulty wiring had led to both of them being severely shocked. Oh, how we grabbed on to this theory! It would not only explain why Christian collapsed but also mean there was nothing wrong with Christian's heart.

John's childhood best friend is an electrician, and we wasted no time asking him to check out the wiring in our home. God bless him, he dropped everything and went immediately. Our hopes grew when he discovered that our home's wiring was backward. He asked me if I'd possibly had a blow dryer on the bathroom counter when Christian collapsed. He seemed to think that if Christian had come in contact with both the blow dryer and the toilet handle simultaneously, he could've gotten quite a jolt. With all of the trauma that morning, which was now more than three weeks past, I had a hard time remembering anything about a blow dryer. I desperately wanted to say yes, but to the best of my recollection, I didn't believe I had.

My journal entry for that day reflected how desperately John and I wanted the cause of Christian's cardiac arrest to be external:

> Oooooh, God! Help us prove beyond doubt that faulty wiring in our house led to Christian being shocked. That would spare him from lifelong ramifications (no defibrillator; no problems with sports or in airports). Ooooh, Lord, with all my heart I am chomping at the bit to write an update that features Ephesians 3:20, "Now all glory to God, who is able, through his mighty power at work within us, to accomplish infinitely more than we might ask or think." Lord, you have already blessed us beyond words, but this external cause would put me over-the-moon! Guide us, Lord, in how to prove it and how to proceed.

Sadly, it was not to be. Upon further investigation, our friend decided our wiring couldn't have been the culprit. Christian's cardiologist confirmed that decision. While he admitted that an electrical shock wasn't impossible, it wasn't likely the cause of Christian's situation. He reasoned that if Christian had been shocked, he typically would've had evidence of burns.

He did not. The cardiologist also said that a shock of that magnitude usually damaged muscles, too. There was no evidence of that from either the lab or urine tests.

Although our high hopes for avoiding the defibrillator were dashed, the Lord was still working overtime on our behalf. And He found a way to buy us more time to learn about defibrillators.

CHAPTER 7

That afternoon, a representative from ZOLL LifeVest® showed up to train us on how to use her product. As the name suggests, it is a vest worn under Christian's shirt. The vest is designed to detect a life-threatening rapid heart rhythm and automatically deliver a treatment to shock the wearer's heart back into its proper rhythm. Along with the vest, Christian wore a small black box containing the battery, slung over one shoulder, which looked like an old-fashioned camera hanging by his side.

I didn't learn until a year later that ZOLL, which does business worldwide, is headquartered in Pittsburgh. We had been told early on that Christian wouldn't leave Children's Hospital without a defibrillator, but this device was our saving grace.

I eventually developed a love/hate relationship with the vest. I'm forever grateful that it bought us time and freedom, but Christian was so thin that even the smallest size didn't fit him snugly enough to work properly. One night, it issued 13 false alarms because when Christian moved in his sleep, the sensors lost contact with his skin.

Those alarms, of course, jolted us out of a sound sleep every time. We eventually started wrapping Ace bandages around the vest, which helped avoid the false alarms. It was a truly blessed night if we endured only one or two false alarms. But the device did have one wonderful benefit: it would help keep Christian safe while he was away from the hospital, which gave us hope that we might be able to temporarily leave the hospital to spend Thanksgiving with our family.

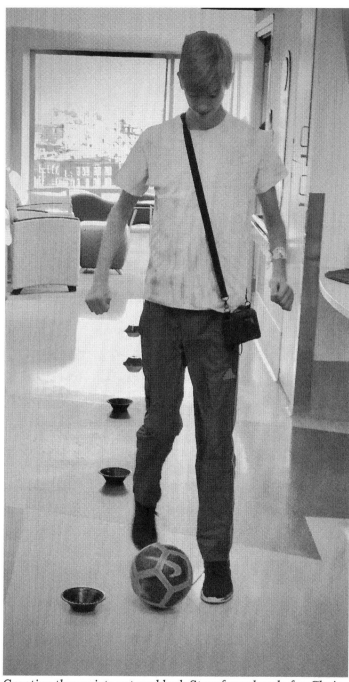

Creative therapists set up black Styrofoam bowls for Christian to practice dribbling the soccer ball around. The black box draped over Christian's shoulder is part of the temporary ZOLL vest.

During our stay in that room, the highlight of Christian's day was physical therapy. His astute therapist quickly learned to incorporate his soccer ball into their sessions. The first photo of Christian that I posted on Facebook since the ordeal began was one of him dribbling a soccer ball down a hospital corridor while he and the therapist laughed. The creative therapist used black Styrofoam bowls as athletic cones and had Christian maneuver the ball in between them. It was sure good medicine for Christian's spirit and this mama's heart.

Even though Christian was progressing well with the many types of therapies he was receiving in the hospital, his dad and I were encouraged to consider sending him to the Children's Hospital Rehabilitation Unit just a few blocks away. The move would enable him to have longer, more frequent sessions with occupational, physical, and speech therapists.

I truly just wanted to bring him home, but it was a nice facility, and we were cautioned that the only way to get there was if he transferred directly from the main hospital. If we brought Christian home first and then discovered he needed more therapy, the opportunity would be lost. I also was swayed heavily by the fact that a teacher there was supposed to work with Christian to help him start on his backlog of schoolwork. So, we agreed to try the rehab, and then awaited an opening for Christian.

John's employer had been phenomenal about allowing him to work from the hospital, but there was one day when he absolutely had to be at the plant. We got word a couple of days before then that the day John had to be at work might be the day Christian would move to the rehab facility. But we weren't too concerned because we'd learned by then that most things at the hospital don't happen when they're scheduled.

Except this one did.

I started gathering and packing our belongings that morning, in case we got the green light to move. Now, after three weeks in the hospital, three people can amass a crazy amount of stuff: laundry (both clean and dirty), a small food pantry, a cooler full of food that friends had brought us, toilet articles, a basket full of get-well cards, a hodgepodge of gifts for Christian including the four giant panels that his basketball coach had instigated, two soccer balls (one used for therapy, one signed by those who'd attended the prayer vigil for Christian), a notebook and paperwork concerning Christian's care, a 10-balloon bouquet and a separate jumbo balloon. And since John was at work, I had no vehicle available.

What ensued would rival a comedic scene from any episode of I Love Lucy.

That morning, I'd expressed my concerns about moving all these items by myself to one of the social workers, and he assured me he would help me move. He also explained that the hospital would get a taxi for me, which was incredibly kind.

Around 2 p.m., we received word that Christian would move that day. I tried multiple times to call/text the social worker but couldn't reach him. Within 30 minutes, an ambulance crew showed up to move Christian. In growing desperation, I convinced them to transport as much of our gear as they could fit onto his gurney, but a small mountain remained. I just wanted to go with Christian, but I had to deal with our worldly goods.

I laboriously filled one luggage cart and maneuvered it down to the hospital lobby, where a security guard agreed to keep an eye on it. Then I began the not-so-simple task of trying to locate a second luggage cart. Time was ticking, I was sweating, and the social worker was still nowhere to be found. I eventually tracked down a second cart and got it loaded up when a nurse took pity on me and escorted me to the lobby using hallways and elevators reserved for employees. That was especially helpful since all the balloons made it incredibly difficult to see where I was driving that thing.

Only then, when I was completely ready to go, would the hospital summon a taxi for me. As I drummed my fingers, waiting impatiently for the taxi, the social worker appeared, full of apologies for being in a meeting and unable to receive my messages. But he didn't bother to stay to help load our possessions into the taxi.

By the time my ride arrived, I was beginning to see the humor in the situation. A female driver emerged, wearing a dress and spiked heels. But she was a trooper, and the two of us worked together to shoehorn a record number of items into her small car. She didn't even know her rear seats would fold down, but thankfully the release was the same as my own car's release, so I knew how to do it. I got the impression she wasn't used to having passengers ride in the front seat with her, but there was no other option. The entire back of her car was loaded to the ceiling, and I even had a few items on my lap and by my feet. Mercifully, the drive to the rehab didn't take nearly as long as it took to pack the taxi.

After being away from home for three weeks and moving to multiple hospital rooms, I'd already been joking about feeling homeless. But when we arrived at the rehab, I burst out laughing when I saw what they provided to transport belongings: grocery carts! I regret that I didn't have the presence of mind to snap a picture of that overstuffed taxi, because only the driver and I know just how much paraphernalia can be crammed into one small car.

We were blessed that Christian was assigned to one of the handful of private rooms in the rehab, but it was still significantly smaller than any of his rooms at the hospital had been. All the rooms in rehab were so small that only one parent could stay each night. Thus began John's introduction to the blessings of the Ronald McDonald House and other Family Houses in Pittsburgh, designed for families of hospital patients. And he even managed to spend a few nights at home in our own bed.

Since we arrived so late in the afternoon, Christian didn't receive any therapies that day, so we spent the evening settling in and exploring our new home. During this rare downtime, I mentioned to Christian that several of his prayer warriors had said, either through cards, texts, or emails, that they knew God had big plans for his life, that He would use Christian's story mightily, etc. When I asked Christian how he felt about that, he said, "Excited!" I was so glad that he was embracing the opportunity.

We had been told that Christian would likely spend two weeks in rehab, so I was bewildered the next morning, before Christian ever met with a single therapist, to find myself in a conference with a tableful of specialists planning for Christian's care after he was discharged. John was patched in via phone, but I felt outnumbered and overwhelmed. In my opinion, Christian was making fantastic progress, but as they went around the table, every expert told me of appointments and therapies he would continue to need after we left the rehab. I just wanted to get my boy home, return to normal life, and tackle the backlog of homework he had missed for the past month.

Ironically, the one person we never saw during Christian's entire stay in the rehab was the teacher who was supposed to help him transition back into school. And her services were one of the main reasons I'd agreed to allow him to go there in the first place. I understood clearly that Christian needed to continue working with a speech therapist after discharge to do exercises to encourage his right vocal cord to work again. And I somewhat understood why they wanted him to take physical therapy, although I thought he could probably do exercises at home.

I kept asking why Christian needed all the other follow-up appointments, what the purpose of them was. I never got much clarity about that. In fact, I was taken aback when one administrator asked me if there was a reason I didn't want my son to get well. But she completely misunderstood me. In her mind, Christian needed these services to recover; in my mind, except for the right vocal cord and regaining his strength, he already was healed.

Although we had some struggles with the administration, all of the therapists who worked with Christian at the rehab were fantastic and beneficial, and the site also proved to be a good transition for him because several of his friends were able to visit him there.

Many of those friends were teammates from his soccer and/or basketball teams. By that time, Christian was feeling well enough that he and his friends played cards or board games, but mostly they kicked a soccer ball around in the hall. A hall with many windows. Large windows. When we were discharged, I was relieved that they hadn't broken any of them.

O ne of those visits turned out to be especially helpful. Two of our adult friends brought two of Christian's buddies to visit him. While the boys practiced their soccer footwork, one mother told us of resources available at the small private school that Christian attended. We were thrilled to learn of a school employee whose job was to coordinate his academic make-up work and see that he got any extra support that he needed.

That knowledge was huge for the first several weeks after Christian eventually returned to school. The other mom had once had a child in the same rehab that Christian was in, and she encouraged us to apply for medical assistance to cover the expenses that were above and beyond what our family's health insurance paid. We never would have thought of doing that, or even realized we were eligible. But through her wisdom, we eventually received that financial help, which was truly a godsend as it saved us thousands of dollars.

I also had an eye-opening experience during their visit. Since one of the ladies is a nurse, John thought she might appreciate seeing pictures he'd taken of Christian early on during his hospitalization, when machines, needles, and other medical paraphernalia completely covered him. As I passed the photos from John to our guest, I glimpsed one of them… and instantly that familiar feeling of my legs going weak returned. While living through the ordeal, God had supernaturally given me the ability to cope with Christian's condition, but now that the crisis had passed, I could no longer handle the reminder.

As Christian plugged away at his daily rehabilitation, it fascinated me to learn how much territory "speech therapy" covered. I remembered having it when I was in second grade and couldn't pronounce the letter "S," but I'm pretty sure that was because I was missing my two front teeth. Christian's speech therapists were much more in-depth. They performed several types of cognitive tests on him to determine how well his memory, concentration, and reasoning were working. I stood behind Christian and mentally took all the tests right along with him. As I later told John, I was thankful they weren't testing me because Christian breezed through the exercises much better than I did!

Because Christian was still at high risk for choking and/or silent aspiration, he still was required to use thickener in all his drinks. By this time, he hated the taste of the thickener so much that he was avoiding drinking. One of the resourceful speech therapists came up with a treatment that she'd never used before, but it gave Christian a bit of respite and helped prevent dehydration. The Frazier Free Water Protocol enabled Christian to have limited amounts of regular water if he took strict precautions. He couldn't drink during or near meals, he was limited to four ounces of water at a time, and he had to thoroughly brush his teeth before drinking so that no particles of food accidentally could get washed into his lungs and cause pneumonia. According to the protocol, even if clear water was aspirated, it would be absorbed into lung tissues without harm. Oh, how he looked forward to those precious sips of unthickened liquid!

It was around this time that it dawned on me that Christian's vocal cord had been damaged after he was anointed with oil, so it wasn't covered by the healing that took place then.

I didn't think my quest to line up a speech therapist for Christian in our community would be too difficult. I had an acquaintance who ran her own speech therapy business, and I assumed we would take him there. However, when I was finally able to contact her—on a mission trip in a foreign country—I was disappointed to learn that she couldn't accept our insurance. I put out a plea to our prayer warriors on Facebook, and they came through big-time! Before I went to bed that night, I was put in contact with a speech therapist near our home who accepted our insurance. As a bonus, her elementary-age daughters attended my son's school, so they already were familiar with his situation, and they had been praying for him! Who could ask for anything better?

B y that time, Thanksgiving was just a few days away, and I still secretly harbored hope that the ZOLL vest would enable Christian to be released for a few hours to celebrate the holiday with our family. But after each of the various types of therapists at the rehab evaluated Christian, we got better news than I ever could have imagined... they set a goal of sending him home! Even though he was initially supposed to stay in the rehab for two weeks, they decided that if he could pass a stress test ordered by one of his doctors, that he should be released a day or two before Thanksgiving.

The earliest time they could arrange the stress test was 1 p.m. on the day before Thanksgiving. John and I had never seen Christian pass up any physical challenge, so we expected he would walk on the treadmill for the longest time possible. We were surprised when he grew tired and asked to end it. But he had walked long enough for the doctor to get the information he needed. The good news was that the results were normal; the bad news was that they shed no light on what had caused Christian's arrhythmia.

We still faced many unknowns. The ZOLL vest was a short-term solution, which bought us some desperately needed time, but it was never designed to be permanent. But at that moment, we didn't care. Our son was alive, alert, his usual funny self... *and* we would be home for the holiday! For the first time in 29 days, we would all sleep in our own beds.

Oh, how I wished that our church still held its annual Thanksgiving Eve service because I was bursting to praise God for all He had done to heal Christian! My urge to give God glory was so strong that I shared a personal story publicly for the first time.

Sixteen years earlier, John and I had attended our church's Thanksgiving Eve service, in which the microphone was open for individuals to share events from the past year for which they were thankful.

At that time, John and I had been trying to have a baby for seven years, but had instead suffered three miscarriages.

But I was so inspired by a recent Christian conference I'd attended and the prayers I'd received there that I boldly shared that God was going to give us a child. A little later in the service, a dear friend stunned me when she shared with the congregation that she believed the Lord was somehow going to use her womb to help me carry a child to term. Neither she nor I had any idea how that was possible, and we never made any attempt to try to figure it out. It wasn't until John and I were driving home that night that I realized how far-fetched some of the things I'd shared had to sound, and I thought, "What have I done?"

A few months later, I *did* get pregnant! As soon as I learned that my due date was in mid-November, my first thought was, "Please, Lord, let the baby be born in time for the Thanksgiving Eve service."

On Thanksgiving Eve 2003, I again walked up to that microphone. Before I ever said a word, those who had attended the previous year burst into applause–I was carrying my two-week-old son. He had been born exactly one year, to the day, from when I'd received prayer at the conference.

Bringing our teenager home from the hospital on that particular date seemed, again, almost as if he'd been reborn. And I was overjoyed that the Lord had chosen to spare my son, especially when He hadn't even spared his own. God's Son, Jesus, died an excruciating death on a cross to pay the price of mankind's sin, returning victoriously to life three days later. Once he conquered death, Jesus eventually returned to heaven to reign with his father, and I fully believe they orchestrated my son's recovery.

Thanksgiving is the one day of the year that John's extended family makes a huge effort to get together. Whenever possible, relatives come from all across the United States and gather at the same enthusiastic cousin's home, which fortunately is fairly near to ours. Normal attendance ranges from the 40s to 60-something. This year, Christian received a hero's welcome as the entire family gave thanks with us for God's mercy. But as we looked around the room, we were struck at just how many family members, some younger than Christian, had their own stories of miraculous healing. Truly, our family was blessed and had much to give thanks for on that Thanksgiving Day and every day.

The only damper on the holiday was when I caught Christian polishing off a 16-ounce bottle of water that hadn't been thickened. And he had no regrets whatsoever about drinking it, insisting that he wasn't choking, and he was safe to drink unthickened beverages. That was when I realized what a challenge awaited when Christian returned to school and wasn't under constant supervision.

Medical personnel had instructed Christian to stay home from school until December 3, when he was allowed to return for half-days. If he was physically and mentally able to handle those, he was permitted to return to full-time classes after a week. That timeline gave Christian 10 days at home between Thanksgiving and his return to classes, but there was no reason to waste valuable time. The day after Thanksgiving, he began the laborious task of making up a month's worth of assignments.

At that time, the first day of rifle season for hunting deer began four days after Thanksgiving in western Pennsylvania. From the time Christian was allowed to participate in mentored hunts, he had joined his dad and uncle in hunting, although he'd never managed to shoot anything. When one of Christian's uncles learned about his cardiac arrest way back in October, that uncle had specifically prayed that Christian would be able to go hunting and that he'd bag his first deer. Christian hunted for a little while that day, although his first deer continued to elude him. But he was physically and mentally able to participate in the annual tradition, and that, all by itself, was evidence of huge progress in his recovery.

CHAPTER 8

As I began to process all that had happened within the past month, I realized that our family had one more thing in common with a Biblical family that played a big role in our lives during the years we were struggling with infertility.

Every time that I became discouraged because I wasn't getting pregnant, some reference would come up to Abraham and Sarah, a couple in the Bible who were unable to have children until the Lord supernaturally blessed them when Abraham was 100 and Sarah was 90-ish. At that time, their son, Isaac, was born.

On the occasional days when I doubted whether God wanted us to have a child, either my devotions would involve Abe and Sarah, or I'd hear a radio program about them, or they'd be the topic of a church sermon. One difficult day, when I was looking up my devotional reading in the New Testament, I thought to myself, "Well, it won't be about Abraham and Sarah today" (because I knew their story was in the Old Testament portion of the Bible). But that day I learned that they are mentioned in the New Testament in Hebrews 11... and that was exactly my devotional reading for the day!

The most dramatic reference to the Biblical couple came on the day I had my third miscarriage. As I lay crying silently on the table, the ultrasound technician, who knew nothing about my history, took my hand and said, "Don't give up, Honey. Remember Abraham and Sarah in the Bible."

John and I so related to Abraham and Sarah that we strongly considered naming our son Isaac. The main reason we didn't is that the word Isaac ends with the same hard "C" sound that our last name begins with. We didn't want him to go through life with his two names running together into one: Isaacater.

But John and I certainly never dreamed that we'd share in Abraham's testing as well. The Bible doesn't specify how old Isaac was when the Lord instructed Abraham to sacrifice him. (God never really intended for Isaac to die: He was testing Abraham's faith and obedience.) I've always pictured Isaac as being a young boy when this happened, but I've now learned that scholars believe his age was somewhere from late teens to early twenties.

As Abraham prepared to kill his beloved son, the Lord provided a ram for him to sacrifice instead. For the most part, while Christian was in the hospital, I never wavered in believing that he would walk out of there fully recovered. But there was one night when I briefly had to ask myself, "What if the Lord chooses not to heal him?" I thought of the lyrics to "Blessed Be Your Name" by Matt Redman, which say in part:

> *You give and take away.*
> *You give and take away.*
> *My heart will choose to say,*
> *Lord, blessed be Your name.*

I asked God to give me the strength to respond that way if I needed to. And that was the end of it.

It wasn't until much later that I realized that, in my own way, I'd had to lay Christian on the altar of sacrifice just as surely as Abraham had. And the Lord was merciful to our family, just as surely as he'd been merciful to Abraham's.

Amid my contemplations, our days fell into a steady rhythm of make-up homework, speech therapy, and physical therapy. But an ominous black cloud hung over me: we could no longer push decisions about a defibrillator to a back burner. Christian was functioning fine in the real world with the external defibrillator in his ZOLL vest, but doctors made it crystal clear that it was only a temporary solution. They insisted he needed a defibrillator implanted in his chest. Soon.

One horrible night, I made the mistake of trying to do Internet research on the two types of possible defibrillators available to Christian. I read awful stories about the side effects of the drugs that accompanied the defibrillators. I was crushed to read of athletes who were no longer able to participate in their sports. Both types of devices had potential life-altering ramifications for their users. I felt certain that the Lord had healed Christian, and I didn't want to saddle him with anything like the contraptions I read about.

The next morning, I wrote in my journal:

> I was reading about life with ICDs last night and I just came unglued. I sobbed because this is NOT the life I want for my son. I have NO peace about this device, but I don't know if that's because you're nudging me away from it or because I don't want to deal with the hassles. Christian's life will change if he gets the device... but at least it's not something like cancer. Does any of my aversion to this stem from pride because my kid won't be "perfect" now? (Not that he ever was!)
>
> After crying my eyes out, I was led to read the book of Job. I have a whole new appreciation for Job's situation and attitude. Lord, when I was reading the Bible, I had peace and I was able to trust you. But as soon as I walked away from it, I was so scared of making the wrong decision that I could have thrown up. God, please help me focus on you today and hear clearly from you. I'm just lost, and I need your help.

Mercifully, our friend and her husband, who works in the defibrillator industry, were available to meet with John and me soon after my misguided attempts to understand defibrillators via the Internet. He was able to put our minds at ease that many improvements had been made over the years, and that much of the information I had read was outdated.

He had been doing some research on our behalf, conferring with one of his competitors about the advantages and disadvantages of each device for Christian's lifestyle, and checking into what doctor would be the best to perform the surgery.

He strongly recommended that his competitor's device, a subcutaneous implantable cardioverter defibrillator (S-ICD), would be better for Christian because he was so young and active. His company's traditional defibrillators are better suited for older patients who also need a pacemaker. One of the major advantages of the S-ICD was that, down the road, it would be easier to remove if deemed unnecessary. Its only drawback was that it was larger than the traditional defibrillator, and since Christian was so thin, the device would protrude through his skin and be easily visible when he's shirtless.

Our friend also was adamant that Christian should not have the surgery performed at Children's Hospital because of his growing six-foot-three-inch frame. He insisted that Christian needed a doctor who was used to working with adults, and he instructed us to contact Dr. Samir Saba.

As tactfully as possible, we asked Christian's doctors at Children's Hospital about the possibility of Dr. Saba implanting the device. They gave us their blessing to contact him but cautioned us of two things: Dr. Saba never sees patients under 18 years of age, and he is so popular that he would be booked for months, while Christian needed the surgery sooner rather than later.

We eventually confirmed that both of those warnings were 100% accurate, but our great and mighty God went before us. Within 45 minutes of my initial call to Dr. Saba's office, the doctor had reviewed Christian's case, decided he could help him, and offered us an appointment just 11 days later. The appointment was at noon, and we suspect he gave up his lunch break that day for us.

We arrived for our appointment with trepidation and a long list of questions. Dr. Saba was so personable and patient that John and I left with sighs of relief. Christian still resisted the whole idea of having surgery. But we all were thrilled to learn that the defibrillator wouldn't prohibit

Christian from participating in activities that he loves, from sports to sledding and from rollercoasters to water slides.

Furthermore, the doctor said he had no plans to put Christian on any of the awful medications I'd read about online unless we discovered that activity caused him problems. And Dr. Saba agreed with our friend that the newer model of defibrillator would be better for Christian's active lifestyle than the more traditional one. He had a son who was Christian's height, and he said that's the device he would've chosen for his child.

After weeks of gut-wrenching dread over deciding about the defibrillator, I could scarcely believe that John and I walked out of Dr. Saba's office with peace. It was a blessed relief.

A midst the drudgery of makeup schoolwork and medical appointments, one glorious, shining night stood out: the season's first basketball game.

Ever since one of Christian's teammates had visited us in the hospital and told us when the first home game was, I had secretly squirreled away the date, hoping upon hope that we might be able to attend. We knew that Christian couldn't play, but John hit upon a brilliant idea to keep him involved with the team. We contacted the coach to see if Christian could help keep the score book, and he readily agreed. When we notified the coach that we planned to attend the first game, he asked us to keep that a secret, saying he wanted Christian's surprise arrival to pump up the team.

But I think the biggest surprise was on us! From the moment we walked into the gym, we were mobbed by friends and school families we'd never met, who had carried us with their prayers and now celebrated with us in Christian's incredible recovery. We arrived at the school plenty early, but I'm pretty sure Christian was late getting to the locker room because so many people greeted him along the way.

As John and I chatted with one well-wisher after another, the pregame music fired up and the team made its usual grand entry, running down a flight of steps and circling the gym. The last person in the line was my son, wearing a team jersey. The coach had even saved his favorite number, 24, for him.

I was already tearing up and overwhelmed with gratitude, but Christian's coach still had a few more surprises up his sleeve. When he prayed before the game, he talked about Christian and gave God all the glory for restoring his health.

As he presented Christian with a jumbo-sized close-up picture of his own face, a bunch of folks in the stands also started waving fan-sized cutouts of Christian's face, which they'd been concealing.

John and I just marveled at how much effort this coach had invested in Christian, especially since Christian was a freshman and new to his team. And we joked about how scary Christian's face was when it was *soooo* big and close up!

Christian didn't keep the book that night; he sat on the bench with his teammates throughout the entire game. And John and I didn't see much of that game because so many people wanted to rejoice with us over Christian's recovery. But we all went home that night feeling incredibly loved and supported.

One question we've heard repeatedly is what caused Christian's cardiac arrest? The bottom-line answer is that we don't know, and we likely never will. But it wasn't for lack of trying. Doctors ran every relevant medical test. A genetic expert worked extensively with medical histories from our extended family, both living and deceased, looking for clues, but came up with nothing significant.

At the basketball team's first game of the season, Coach Matt Harbison, left, publicly praises the Lord for healing Christian. One of his teammates, Elijah White, right, holds a fan with Christian's picture on it.

A prophetic friend said the Lord showed her that a tick had bitten Christian the summer before when we visited Yellowstone National Park and that triggered the cardiac arrest. Although no medical tests were ever able to confirm that, it was a relief to me to think it was a onetime occurrence rather than a lifelong threat. But truthfully, the reassurance that gave me the most peace was our pastor's words not to be surprised if we never found out what caused it because the Lord healed completely. Those are words I latched on to when I first heard them and continue to draw strength and comfort from today.

We have told Christian point blank, though, that we believe there was a spiritual battle for his life. We believe the devil tried to kill him and the Lord said *no*. Since the cardiac arrest, I have learned stories of several Christian leaders who nearly died when they were young. Only time will tell if the enemy was trying to eliminate Christian because of whatever plans God has for his future.

One astounding discovery that we try to share with others is that sudden cardiac arrest (SCA) is *not* rare! Because cardiac arrest claims seemingly healthy victims so suddenly, mourners tend to write off their death as a tragic fluke. However, The American Heart Association's *CPR Facts & Stats* reports that 475,000 Americans die annually from cardiac arrest. Worldwide, it claims more lives than colorectal cancer, breast cancer, prostate cancer, influenza, pneumonia, auto accidents, HIV, firearms, and house fires *combined*.

Cardiac arrest is no respecter of persons. In the year or so following Christian's brush with death, we personally knew of four people it had claimed, ranging from a five-year-old boy to a 30-something man and a middle-aged woman. The one that hit home the most, though, was a high school athlete whose basketball team our boys had played just a few weeks before he died.

Parent Heart Watch, a national organization whose goal is to protect youth from sudden cardiac arrest, asserts that SCA is the #1 killer of student athletes and the leading cause of death on school campuses. The group's Web site, parentheartwatch.org, promotes awareness, preventative screenings, and training with the goal of eliminating preventable deaths from sudden cardiac arrest by 2030. Christian's case wouldn't have been considered preventable because he didn't have a preexisting condition, but the screenings could benefit the one in 300 youth with an undetected heart condition that puts them at risk.

Parent Heart Watch is pushing for a mandatory national registry to track cardiac arrests in youth. The hope is that such a registry would promote new research and strategies to help prevent sudden cardiac deaths. As it stands, estimates of the number of youth stricken annually range from 7,000 to 23,000

Back on the home front, as we prepared for Christian to return to school, I was confident he was ready physically, but I had a major concern about whether he would follow the hated rules regarding thickening all liquids he consumed. Hoping to have other eyes checking on him when I couldn't, I sent the following letter to the mothers of his classmates:

Hi, Moms:

I'm recruiting your kids—Christian's classmates—to help him make a safe return to school. On Monday, he'll be back for half-days, but he'll spend the whole first week in the resource room. On Dec. 10, we're hoping he's caught up enough to return to regular classes full-time.

It is both a blessing and a curse that Christian has no memory of his roughest days in the hospital. Because he FEELS 100% fine right now, he tends to not take his therapies seriously and tries to cut corners. Your kids could be a huge help in applying positive peer pressure if they see him drinking anything that's not thickened. In other words, no sips from the water fountain, no Dr. Pepper or any other pop (unless it's thickened, but it tastes awful), etc. The ONLY exception is that, once he's back full-time, he will be allowed four ounces of regular water right BEFORE lunch... but ONLY if it is carefully measured and if he has brushed his teeth thoroughly for two minutes beforehand.

Because Christian's right vocal cord isn't working, he runs two risks if he ignores these instructions: He risks choking, and he also risks putting bacteria in his lungs, which could lead to pneumonia (again). Testing at the hospital showed that even when it appeared that he was swallowing OK, he was aspirating silently.

It is very much a hassle for him, and I understand why he balks at doing it, but it is for his own safety. This will last until he passes another swallow test, which won't be ordered until Dec. 18 AT THE EARLIEST.

By the way, he has very few limitations on what foods he can eat (although I will continue to push the healthy ones)! He's not allowed to eat anything that would be too liquidy, such as ice cream, soup, and juicy fruits, such as mandarin oranges, watermelon, grapefruit, and grapes.

Your kids also deserve to have a basic understanding of the special vest that Christian is wearing under his shirt. They won't see it, but they'll see the black box attached to it that he wears slung over his shoulder. He looks like a tourist carrying an old-fashioned camera.

This vest/box is an external defibrillator, which means that if his heart gets out of rhythm like it did when he had the cardiac arrest, it will sense that and automatically shock his heart back into rhythm. (Picture the old TV shows where doctors used paddles to shock people whose hearts had stopped; this device does that all by itself.)

THE MOST IMPORTANT THING your kids need to know is not to touch Christian if he is receiving a treatment. They, too, would get shocked. If he collapses again, the ONLY thing they need to do is call 911. I'm not trying to scare anybody, and I truly hope this isn't ever an issue, but your kids should know what to do. Knowledge is power.

Now, his device makes two different noises. The loud, urgent one should occur only if Christian is having a heart problem. (We haven't had it sound yet, but we've heard the alarm during training sessions.) If it sounds and he's fine, he knows how to program the box so he doesn't get an unneeded shock treatment.

Your kids very likely may hear the other noise, which sounds like the ding that an elevator door makes when it opens. We've heard this one MANY times, and it just means that something within the device isn't making proper contact with his skin. It used to go off every night while he was sleeping until we started wrapping him with Ace bandages to hold it tight to his skin. (He's too thin for even the smallest vest.) The black box will tell him which sensor(s) need to be adjusted. He may be able to fix it during class or he may need to go to the nurse's office for a little help. Since we started wrapping him, we've had minimal incidents.

I'm sending this to all the parents for whom I have contact information, either by email or texting. Please feel free to share with any others you are aware of.

I can't say it enough, THANK YOU for all your prayers and other support for our family during the past 5+ weeks. There's no doubt in our minds that your prayers carried us and made a difference, and we feel so blessed to be part of such a caring school community.

If you have any questions, please feel free to ask!

After sending out that letter, I was touched to learn that the school nurse already had taken the initiative to learn about the ZOLL vest and share her knowledge with Christian's teachers. The stage was set for Christian's return to school. I had been working with him at home on the subjects that I could, but I was more than happy to hand him off to real teachers to help him with geometry and science.

CHAPTER 9

C hristian soared through his week of half-days, and everyone agreed he was ready to return full time. As Christian climbed onto the bus on the morning of December 10, I breathed a sigh of relief. For the first time in nearly seven weeks, our family had a normal day, with John going to work and Christian off to school. Only seven weeks? It seemed like a lifetime had gone by.

We continued to see God working on our behalf when Dr. Saba's scheduler called to set a date for Christian's defibrillator surgery. When we had seen the doctor, we had requested that the surgery take place during Christmas break. I didn't want Christian to have to miss any more school; my practical husband wanted the surgery before the end of the year since we'd already more than met our insurance deductible. Dr. Saba had told us that he was going to be out of the country for Christmas, flying home on December 26. So, we were overjoyed to learn he had slotted us for a very early appointment on December 27.

As grateful as we were for Dr. Saba's compassion, something still nagged in the back of my mind. If God had truly healed Christian, were we displaying a lack of trust by having the device implanted? John and I wrestled with that question right up until the day of Christian's surgery. We consulted with Christian friends who unanimously said we should proceed with the implant. John realized that if Christian didn't have the defibrillator implanted, no doctor in his right mind would ever authorize him to play sports.

We ultimately put out a fleece to God, meaning we asked for a specific sign that only God could arrange. We were 100% prepared to cancel the surgery and walk by faith if the Lord gave us this sign. To be honest,

I expected Him to. Although the drawbacks to the defibrillator weren't nearly as life-altering as I'd initially feared, if Christian had the surgery, he would deal with the effects for the rest of his life.

While we waited on the Lord's sign, we continued our merry-go-round of speech therapy, physical therapy, and homework while attempting to prepare for Christmas. Since Christian's birthday had been such a dud, I wanted to make sure that Christmas was extra special.

As it turned out, a doctor gave Christian a better early Christmas present than anything I could've bought at a store. He was still using the thickener, which he loathed, in everything he drank—at least when he was around me. I strongly suspect he was cheating on the requirements when he wasn't under my supervision. But his instructions were to use the thickener until his vocal cord healed. Unfortunately, the only way we could know if that occurred was for him to undergo the same horrid test he'd had in the hospital, which originally showed his right vocal cord wasn't working. We grudgingly agreed that he needed the test, but I was adamant that it would not be administered by the same doctor.

We were referred to an ear, nose, and throat specialist at Children's Hospital who turned out to be wonderful. The test was still awful, but she explained everything that was going to happen and empowered Christian to have some say in the procedure. And the results were worth the discomfort! Although the right vocal cord was not completely healed, it was well on the road to recovery and the doctor expected it to finish healing on its own with time. That meant, hallelujah, that Christian could discontinue using the thickener!

Our first stop on the way home was a milkshake to celebrate. And when we got home, Christian had a date with his favorite doctor: Dr. Pepper! He had received a bottle of his favorite soft drink as a gift when he was in the hospital, and he'd been saving it until he could enjoy it without thickener.

Since the speech therapy had accomplished its goal, Christian no longer needed to see that therapist or do voice exercises every day. And the next week, after just eight sessions, the physical therapist also released Christian.

A major milestone! Christian is allowed to discontinue using thickener in all his drinks. Of all the doctors he encountered, Dr. Pepper was his favorite.

A midst all the medical appointments, there was one meeting that Christian had his heart set on attending. Every year, a group from his school takes a mission trip to the Dominican Republic to help the impoverished people there with medical and vision care, construction work, Vacation Bible Schools, prayer, and recreation. Christian had participated the year before and desperately wanted to return.

At the time he'd collapsed, he already had signed up to go on the trip, but as he lay in the induced coma at the hospital, I'd thought to myself, "There is no way on earth I'm letting him go to a developing country now."

As Christian recovered, his interactions with the doctors were limited mainly to answering their questions. There was only one subject that motivated Christian enough to initiate a conversation: could he still go to the Dominican Republic? Much to my surprise, doctor after doctor told him yes. I was still very dubious about the trip. I was willing to take Christian to the first group meeting about it, and we agreed to keep working toward the trip as long as God kept opening the doors for him to go. But Christian conceded that if God closed the door, he would accept it.

When we arrived for the meeting, the group leader pulled me aside and asked if I'd looked at Christian's online account balance. I hadn't because I'd had no reason to do so. He explained that an anonymous donor had already paid for Christian's trip! I was so stunned, my initial response was, "What happens if Christian doesn't wind up going?" The leader wisely told me we'd cross that bridge if we got to it. But the more I contemplated the donor's generosity, I came to believe that God used that person to make it clear to John and me that He wanted Christian to go on the mission trip. And that Christian would be fine.

The speech and physical therapy sessions ended the week before Christmas, and I was wonderfully relieved to not have to wedge four appointments into each week's calendar.

The way was clear for us to celebrate a joyous and thankful Christmas, which we did, but Christian's surgery still loomed over our heads.

On Christmas morning, I wrote in my journal:

> This is my "grateful Christmas." Lord, I know they all should be, but sitting at our church's Candlelight Service last night, I felt just like I did 15 years ago: Grateful to have my son for Christmas.

Most of our family members live out-of-state, so to celebrate a typical Christmas, we either travel to visit some of them or they come to stay with us. But because of Christian's surgery, neither of those options was possible. We wound up having a lovely Christmas with the handful of relatives who live nearby, but it was by far the quietest Christmas I'd had since John and I got married.

The day after Christmas, I looked forward to a visit from a high school friend, now living in New Jersey, who had come home to western Pennsylvania for the holiday. She and I had both had our children later in life, and our kids were only three months apart in age. We had such a fun time with her family that it was easy to not think about the impending surgery. By the time they left, it was time for John, Christian, and me to head to Pittsburgh.

I was genuinely surprised when it was time to go that God had not sent any messages in response to our fleece. After all I had seen God bring Christian through so far, I was just sure he would spare him from needing the surgery. Yet no signs had come. I headed out with disappointment, but also with peace.

Because Christian needed to be at the hospital at 6:15 the next morning, we opted to spend the night in Pittsburgh, so we didn't have an hour-long drive in the wee hours. Happily, the Ronald McDonald House had an opening, so we were able to stay there. We passed the evening watching TV, exchanging silly texts with family members, and generally trying to keep Christian's mind off the surgery. He insisted that he didn't need the defibrillator, and he also was very afraid of what lay ahead. He made several comments about dying during the surgery.

The next morning, we arrived at the designated waiting room before it was even unlocked. After all the required paperwork and pre-operational preparations were made, they wheeled my baby away. Oh, how I wished I could've taken his place.

John and I had a long wait ahead of us, so we deposited our packed lunches in the waiting room and set out walking the halls to try and get our 10,000 steps in that day. After we'd walked for about an hour, we decided to head back to the waiting room. As we approached it, we saw a security guard and his trained dog enter the room. I joked that I hoped the dog didn't eat my lunch. As it turned out, our unattended lunches had raised someone's suspicions and they had called security to make sure there was nothing dangerous in our small cooler and brown bag. We all had a good laugh, and it gave us a funny story to entertain Christian with later.

Christian's surgery went smoothly, and Dr. Saba was delighted that he'd been able to devise a new way to insert the defibrillator so that it stuck out as minimally as possible on Christian's thin frame. It was still plainly visible, but not nearly as much as the doctor had initially expected.

The surgery and recovery went so well that the biggest glitch of the day was that the TV in Christian's room didn't work. His beloved Pittsburgh Penguins had a game that night that he was looking forward to watching. His nurse racked up all kinds of brownie points when she allowed him to go to a nearby lounge to view the game. And when he went to bed that night, for the first time in more than a month, he did so without the threat of the ZOLL vest going off accidentally. The vest that had given us freedom and bought us time was no longer needed.

Christian was discharged the next morning with instructions to take it easy for a few days. Since school was still closed for Christmas vacation, several of Christian's friends were able to visit him at our house, and he even had a few boys spend the night on New Year's Eve, ringing in what we fervently hoped would be a healthier year.

Christian also spent much time in his continued efforts to catch up on homework and tests from the month he'd been absent. The teacher for his Bible class even made a house call, giving Christian personal instruction in the class work he'd missed. It was not lost on me what a blessing it was that Christian's recovery period included both Thanksgiving and Christmas breaks, which gave him a chance to catch up while not having to simultaneously be keeping up with new material.

Thanks to Dr. Saba's willingness to fit Christian's surgery in during December, by the time school resumed after Christmas vacation, Christian was ready to go. Ten days after Christian left the hospital, he had a follow-up appointment with Dr. Saba. Everything looked great, and Dr. Saba pronounced instructions that were music to our ears and we have readily embraced, "Go live a normal life."

Four days later, Christian left with our church youth group to attend a weekend retreat. He was supposed to take it pretty easy, but he took a few careful runs on the sledding hill, thankfully, with no ill effects. When we learned Christian was able to go to the retreat, John and I made reservations for a much-needed, months-overdue getaway at a local motel with a swimming pool and hot tub... but God had a different idea.

We were invited to share Christian's story of the miraculous power of prayer with the prayer team from a nearby church. John and I were so torn. We desperately needed a break after three draining months, but we longed to give God all the glory we could for saving our son. We couldn't change the date of our weekend away, and the prayer team couldn't change its meeting date. In the end, John and I agreed to interrupt our all-too-short getaway to drive to the church to tell Christian's story.

I believe we were asked to share for ten to 15 minutes, but we did the world's worst job of time management. John began the talk, and almost immediately broke into tears. Telling the story aloud proved very therapeutic for him, and our listeners responded with grace and love. After we wrapped up the story, a couple of women from the group prophesied that we would have many more opportunities to share Christian's story and that it would be one of many that the Lord would use to help bring revival to America. That was hard for us to fathom since we're just a typical middle-class family, but we left there, after about an hour, willing to share it as often as we could.

The following week brought midterms and the end of the second grading period. Our goal all along was to be completely caught up by that time, and the school official who coordinated Christian's makeup work assured us that he was. When report cards came out shortly thereafter, we were dumbfounded that he received an incomplete in Spanish, which had been the very first assignments he had made up.

Through a small snafu, there were a couple of papers that he'd never been given, but he easily completed them within a day. It was a huge relief to have the monkey of make-up work off our backs! And his grades were remarkably consistent with the ones he'd earned in the first nine-week grading period, before his cardiac arrest. The biggest difference was that, during the grading period when he missed six weeks of school, his geometry grade improved by ten points!

By the end of January, Christian was due for a brain injury assessment at Children's Hospital. His mind was working so normally that I didn't believe he needed it. And I was less than thrilled that he would need to miss an entire afternoon of school to attend since no appointments are available after school hours. In the end, we went, mainly because the rehab administrator's words still rang in my ears: "Is there a reason you don't want your son to get well?"

Our appointment completely vindicated how I'd felt all along and proved God's goodness. We had been told to expect a three-hour appointment with a variety of doctors assessing different aspects of Christian's recovery. He breezed through their questions and exchanged enough good-natured banter with one doctor that Christian and that doctor wound up having a footrace down the hospital hall... and Christian won! After a few more assessments, the doctor asked for a rematch. That time the doctor won, but they had been in a dead heat until Christian's shoe came off. Even with two footraces, we left the hospital in less than an hour, happily, with zero requests for further assessments.

About that time, John and I attended our first worship night at a neighboring church. We had assumed it would last only one hour, so when it ran significantly longer, we whispered about cutting out early. But the music and prayers were so powerful, we couldn't bring ourselves to leave. And we were richly rewarded. The very last song of the night, "Raise a

Hallelujah," was one we had never heard, yet its lyrics perfectly described the role of worship music in Christian's healing.

> *I raise a hallelujah, in the presence of my enemies*
> *I raise a hallelujah, louder than the unbelief*
> *I raise a hallelujah, my weapon is a melody*
> *I raise a hallelujah, Heaven comes to fight for me*
>
> *I'm gonna sing, in the middle of the storm*
> *Louder and louder, you're gonna hear my praises roar*
> *Up from the ashes, hope will arise*
> *Death is defeated, the King is alive!*
>
> *I raise a hallelujah, with everything inside of me*
> *I raise a hallelujah, I will watch the darkness flee*
> *I raise a hallelujah, in the middle of the mystery*
> *I raise a hallelujah, fear, you lost your hold on me!*
>
> *I'm gonna sing, in the middle of the storm*
> *Louder and louder, you're gonna hear my praises roar*
> *Up from the ashes, hope will arise*
> *Death is defeated, the King is alive!*

I was completely overwhelmed by the song, to the point that I couldn't even sing. I simply wept, especially over the lines that said, "I raise a hallelujah, my weapon is a melody; I raise a hallelujah, Heaven comes to fight for me." In hindsight, that was exactly what the Lord had done through the praise music that He had prompted us to play while Christian was in the hospital.

I was so blown away by the song that I went home and tried to find out the story behind it. The back story sounded eerily familiar: a young boy life-flighted to a Children's Hospital, on the brink of death. His parents were somehow associated with Bethel Music from Bethel Church in Redding, California, and in the middle of the ordeal, worship team members Jonathan David Helser, Melissa Helser, and Molly Skaggs wrote this declaration of triumph. The little boy made a full recovery!

More than a year later, I found out more details about the boy and
his family: Bethel Music CEO Joel Taylor and his wife, Janie, took their
two-year-old son Jaxon to the hospital with what they thought was a
normal child's illness. The Taylors soon discovered that Jaxon's kidneys
were shutting down due to an E. coli virus attacking his organs.

The morning after I first heard the song, I just had to share the news with
our prayer warriors on Facebook. I wrote:

> For those who followed Christian's saga, you won't be at all
> surprised that the Lord gave me a new song last night. I'd never
> heard "Raise a Hallelujah" by Bethel Music, but it captivated me
> because it perfectly describes how we got through Christian's
> ordeal. I did a little research that brought me to tears: It was
> written because a couple's son was in intensive care last month
> and not expected to make it … yet he, like Christian, made a
> miraculous recovery.

> I truly can't explain the role that music played in Christian's
> recovery. All I know is that while we waited for doctors to stabilize
> him at Children's Hospital, we worshiped through songs. During
> that time, we were impressed to play praise music continually
> in Christian's room. Almost daily, the Lord gave John and me
> different songs to lean on. I surrendered my son to God while
> repeatedly playing Laura Story's "Blessings," and when conditions
> were at their worst, I praised God through exhausted tears. Even
> though it was the last thing in the world I felt like doing, the very
> act of obedience gave me the strength to go on and a new sense
> of hope.

> One of this new song's lyrics that struck me the most was about
> the need to sing "in the middle of the storm." Christian's situation
> was many times compared to a storm, but your storm may have
> nothing to do with health. It could be anything that causes
> turbulence in your life: job, finances, marriage issues, prodigal
> children, addiction. You name it. I believe the concept of praising

God during the battle, as the song suggests, will influence the outcome. What a crazy, freeing, mind-boggling relief to realize that our singing unleashes God to fight our battles for us.

CHAPTER 10

B y early February, life had returned to normal enough that I had time to make good on a vow I'd made on Day One, while John and I were driving to the hospital. It was still unconscionable to me that it had taken so long for an ambulance to reach our home the day Christian collapsed.

For months, we told people that the ambulance had taken 20 minutes to get to our house—and truthfully it seemed much longer than that—but when we contacted the 911 center to confirm the timeline, we were surprised that the ambulance had arrived in "only" 13 minutes. Still, I was determined to find out why it took so long and do all I could to make sure such a delayed response never happened again.

I started with the fire chief in the town nearest to our rural township. He patiently and kindly filled me in on the problems plaguing the ambulance industry in our area. He explained that one of our community's two ambulance services had closed, and the remaining one had trouble finding emergency responders because the pay was so low.

On top of that, he cited people who abused the system by using an ambulance for personal transportation. He told me of people who called 911 to request an ambulance, rode to the hospital, and then, without ever entering the hospital, got out and walked to their nearby destination. He also said that when people need ambulances to transport them between medical facilities, that reduces the number available for emergency responses. He told me that one day, by 8 a.m., all ambulances in the county were already tied up on non-emergency runs.

The fire chief was very painfully aware of the gaps in our community's ambulance coverage, and he had been in contact with local and state politicians to find ways to improve the situation. Sadly, nothing was progressing very quickly, and I shuddered to think of how many people would die needlessly before action was taken.

The only encouraging news the chief was able to give me was that most of his firefighters have medical training and carry the automated external defibrillators, or AEDs, that Christian so desperately needed to shock his heart back into rhythm and save his life. But I learned, too late, that when we called 911, we had to specifically request that the fire department respond. I vaguely recall the 911 operator asking if I wanted him to send the fire department, and I naively declined.

In my ignorance, I believe that I said, "No, my house isn't on fire." Without my requesting the firefighters, a Pennsylvania law prohibits them from responding into a different jurisdiction unless they are dispatched by the 911 center, even if they could save lives. In our case, the fire chief remembered my frantic 911 call and told me he lives five minutes from our home and keeps an AED in his vehicle.

I also spoke with a local state representative who had been trying to address the ambulance shortage, but more than three years after Christian collapsed, I still see no significant changes. The most likely way to successfully improve the system would be with a small tax that would go directly to emergency responders. I despise taxes as much as the next person, but this is one that I would support and work to get approved.

As long as my family continues to live in our current home, I know that we risk not having an ambulance available when we need it. And if we ever move, one of the key things I'd look for in a new home is reliable ambulance service.

While I was getting a crash course in ambulance woes, Christian had a laser focus on returning to playing sports. Once Christian's post-surgery recovery time was complete and his class work was all made up, the stage was set for him to return to basketball practice on Saturday, February 2. We all had been looking forward to that day for weeks, but we hit one last-minute snag.

The day before his scheduled return, I got word late in the afternoon that he needed a permission slip signed by a doctor or the school couldn't let him practice. I quickly called Dr. Saba's office. Even though Dr. Saba wasn't in his office that afternoon, and even though they were dealing with a medical emergency, his assistants worked some magic and they faxed the required permission slip to the school's athletic director, who thankfully was working late that day. The boy was good to go!

After just a week of practice, Christian got to play a little in the final game of the regular season. When our teams make their grand entrances for each game, they run down a long flight of steps from the locker room to the gym floor, with music blaring and fans cheering.

As Christian ran down those steps, I flashed back to a message I'd received when Christian was in the hospital from a teammate's parent. It said, "I had a dream of your son Saturday night. He and I were walking down steps into a large auditorium and when we landed on the last few steps, I realized it was a basketball court. Christian ran out onto the court fully dressed for the game and ready to play!!" I had clung to that prophetic dream throughout Christian's recovery and was simply overwhelmed with gratitude to God that it had come true.

Christian played a little in the junior varsity game that night and scored one basket, and he even saw a bit of playing time in the varsity game.

As momentous as Christian's return to playing basketball was, something even more significant occurred that night. At long last, we got the answer that helped us understand why the doctor and nurse had described Christian as a miracle based on what they'd seen in the EKGs taken when he was still on our bathroom floor. EKGs and ECGs, two abbreviations for the same procedure, both refer to electrocardiograms, which measure electrical activity and collect data on heart health.

One of Christian's former coaches is an associate professor at Slippery Rock University. Before working at SRU, he was a visiting professor at the University of Toledo, where he taught about reading EKGs. After confirming his interpretations with SRU colleagues currently teaching about EKGs, he explained to us that people suffer irreparable brain damage if they are without oxygen for eight minutes or don't have a heartbeat for 20 minutes.

Between the amount of time John and the paramedics performed CPR on Christian and then used the defibrillator, he wasn't breathing and didn't have a heartbeat of his own for between 27½ and 31½, depending on how the EKG is interpreted. For the first time, we began to get a glimpse of just how much of a miracle Christian's recovery was.

The very next night, we were blown away even more. I had signed all three of us up to take a CPR class that included instruction on using the defibrillators that hang on the walls in public buildings. The instructor had no idea what our family had just gone through or why we were taking the class. She explained to the group the importance of quickly getting a defibrillator to anyone in cardiac arrest. She said that for each minute that elapses without the defibrillator, the person's chances of survival decrease by ten percent.

"So," she said bluntly, "After ten minutes, they're dead."

My eyes teared up at the magnitude of her words. But as I contemplated what she'd said, frankly, I didn't believe her. I mean, Christian was sitting right there, and his heart had been stopped for nearly three times that long. I thought she had to have her statistics wrong. I went home that night and did some research on the Internet. I found multiple sites with multiple sources that all confirmed the instructor's information.

Only then, nearly four months after Christian collapsed, did John and I finally begin to grasp exactly how much of a miracle the Lord had given us. Many months later, when John and I were looking closely at Christian's EKGs, we noticed for the first time two places where the words "agonal rhythm" were handwritten. Out of curiosity, John Googled the term, and the search results floored us.

The first item John found was in a blog post by Dr. Nabil Paktin, a consultant and clinical cardiologist, who wrote, "An agonal rhythm is from a dying heart and is 99+% of the time, not recoverable." John also discovered a curriculum for nursing students at RN.com which said that agonal rhythm is seen in the late stages of unsuccessful resuscitation attempts. When patients reached that stage, the manual advised nurses to consider termination of efforts so they could turn their attention to supporting the patient's family.

From time to time, I overheard Christian's classmates making statements that began "when Christian died" or "after Christian died." Those comments always amused me, but those teens actually grasped what had happened with Christian better than I did. We eventually tracked down the emergency responders who had helped him survive, because we wanted to thank them. One of them explained that they considered Christian "clinically dead" or "dead with resuscitative efforts" during the time his heart wasn't beating.

Clinical death is the medical term for cessation of blood circulation and breathing, the two criteria necessary to sustain the lives of human beings.

We are forever grateful that none of Christian's emergency medical technicians or doctors gave up on him! And all those prayers from all those people all around the world truly were answered.

T here was little time to ponder these mindboggling realizations because the basketball team was headed to the playoffs. Christian was relegated back to the bench for these important games, but he continued practicing with the team and getting stronger. The boys earned a spot in the championship game, which featured the wildest comeback I've ever witnessed. Our team led for most of the first half but was losing by 16 at the beginning of the fourth quarter. Following a scoring frenzy, with two seconds on the clock, our team tied the score to send the game into overtime. We ultimately won by 12 points. I was so glad that Christian was able to be a part of that experience! Even though he didn't play in that game, his day was coming.

Two weeks later, our school hosted a tournament for basketball players in grades ten and under. As each game progressed, Christian kept playing a little more and a little more. But John and I were still shocked when the starters were introduced for the championship game... and Christian was the only freshman on our team with four sophomores! We figured he would just play for a few minutes and then be replaced. Honestly, we didn't know how much stamina he had built up yet. But the clock kept ticking and Christian was still on the court. He played nearly the entire game, and his team won the tournament for the first time under his coach's tutelage. I know his coach fervently wanted to win that game, so he wasn't letting Christian play just to be nice; Christian had earned that spot.

A couple of days later, it hit me that the young man who had started the basketball season in a coma had finished it as a starter on a championship team. To God be the glory!

During that period, both our church and Christian's school offered CPR classes. I don't know that they were inspired by Christian's case per se, but I do know that several people who took the classes did so because of what had happened to Christian. A nurse at Christian's school requested permission to share his story in the CPR class that she routinely taught for eighth graders, and we readily agreed. We are thankful for any way that the Lord can use Christian's experience to help others.

The next big event on Christian's calendar was the long-awaited, much-anticipated mission trip with his school friends to the Dominican Republic. Christian was chomping at the bit to go, and the Lord gave me perfect peace about it. Several moms empathized with me that it must be hard to let Christian go so far away after what we'd just been through. But I had to tell them that I was honestly doing fine. I figured that if God hadn't taken Christian home five months ago, when He very easily could have, He wasn't going to do it now.

Deep down, I'd hoped that Christian might share his testimony with some of the people in the Dominican. He never brought it up at home, and only reluctantly discussed it if someone else did. I knew it was powerful and could encourage a lot of people. But I also was thankful to a friend who had survived a sudden cardiac arrest when he was in his late 30s. He told John and me that he couldn't bring himself to talk about it for three years. And I imagine it's even harder for a teenager to come to grips with than an adult.

In the end, Christian didn't wind up sharing his story during the trip. But his journey was still incredibly worthwhile. He took notes and wrote his thoughts throughout the week to share with the anonymous benefactor who had paid for his trip. (The group leader agreed to relay Christian's thank-you letter to the donor, whose identity we still don't know.) I was blown away by the deep emotions that Christian described in his letter because we never, and I mean never, see any evidence of these at home. I joked to John that the thoughts expressed were so insightful that I'd have been tempted to think Christian copied them from the Internet, if it weren't for the misspelled words.

A few snippets of Christian's writings (with a little help from Mom on spelling and punctuation) included:

> This is the last day I will get to serve these people in their great land. Today is the last day I'll get to wake up and know that I have a chance to change someone's life. Today is the last day where I can get to pass a soccer ball to a little kid and have him mock my Spanish. Today is the last day where I can get up and realize that it's time to get over myself and my own pity party and that there are people way worse off than me.

> It has been sooooo amazing learning from all these wonderful Christians who have nothing but still trust in God better than we (Americans) do. It's amazing how close some people become when they spend a week with each other. It has been wonderful to see how much of a difference it makes when many believers all seek the same goals for the same reasons and don't worry about the petty quarrels of the Western church. When everyone is united in one purpose, that is when the glory of God will shine through.

One thing that God has impressed on my heart this week is that the Dominican isn't the only place we can serve God. If you set your mind on God, you can be a missionary in your workplaces, schools, or even sports teams or clubs. Shortly, I'll be leaving my carefree home-away-from-home for the trials of my actual home. This year, however, I am ready for whatever the enemy will throw at me, through God's help.

I hear certain people at school who say, 'Why would I go spend $1,000 to help someone I've never met?' I never really had an answer to that until last night when I realized that that is only part of what the trip is about. Yes, helping make the world a better place and spread the love of Jesus is definitely a big part of it, but it's also helpful for yourself. When you see how happy people are with nothing, how caring people are when no one cares for them, and how loving people are when it seems the world doesn't love them, it shows how much more happy, caring, and loving we, as blessed Americans, should be to others.

The two words kinda given to me this week were 'unconditional love.' I wasn't really sure what that meant at first, but I kinda figured it out as the week went on. To me at least, unconditional love meant that I had one week to give as much hope, love, joy, and Jesus to all the little kids that I saw. So, even when I felt tired or just wasn't feeling like doing anything, I would say the words 'unconditional love' as kind of a motivational thing to remind me of Christ's unconditional love and how great it would be if I, even in a small part, could share God's love with people who needed to hear it.

This has been one of, if not the best, weeks of my life. Even with the struggles and fighting through the tiredness, this has been so rewarding and I have to come back next year, even if it costs me my last dime. God moves so mightily in the Dominican, but all we need to do is show up and let God flow through us.

I'm feeling motivated because I feel sorta more clearly that this would be something I would be able to do with my life and definitely enjoy... I love the people there and hope to be able to come back as long as God allows me to come. The Dominican Republic has been placed heavily on my heart and, who knows, maybe I'll work there someday.

This week, I found something meaningful and helpful to serve God's kingdom that I love to do. If that's not a purpose, I don't know what is.

Yes, based on Christian's observations, I'd say he absolutely was meant to serve on that mission team.

Christian plays a hand game with one of his Dominican friends.

Left: The mission team plays volleyball with the neighborhood residents.
Top right: Christian plays the part of Noah in a Bible story
presented to children in the Dominican Republic.
Bottom right: Christian enjoys his beloved soccer with locals.

PHOTOS THIS PAGE ARE COURTESY OF COCO HOFFER PHOTOGRAPHY.

CHAPTER 11

About the time Christian received his defibrillator, I stumbled across an ad on YouTube for a movie called *Breakthrough*, which was due to be released in a few months. It was based on the true story of a teenage boy who fell through the ice on a lake and was lifeless for more than an hour... until his mother, Joyce Smith, prayed over him in the emergency room and his heart started beating again. The parallels to Christian's story overwhelmed me, and I couldn't even listen to the entire commercial.

A few weeks later, John spotted the same advertisement and played it for me. That time, I was able to get through the entire preview. It still rattled me pretty badly, but I knew beyond any doubt that we would go see the movie.

By the time my birthday rolled around in late February, I was delighted when a friend gave me a book called *The Impossible*, which recounted the entire story upon which the movie was based. I hadn't even known that a book was available about the boy in the movie, but I read the entire story in one sleepless night. More than ever, the similarities between the two boys' ordeals jumped out at me, both in the big details as well as many smaller ones.

On the day before Easter, about four months after Christian received his defibrillator, John and I took him and two of his friends to see the movie. Christian was reluctant to go, but we thought it might help him and his friends understand what he had gone through and better grasp how much the Lord had done to restore him.

The next day, Easter morning, I posted on Facebook:

We celebrated this Resurrection Day last night by seeing the movie 'Breakthrough.' The story of a boy who falls into an ice-covered lake has many parallels to what Christian experienced with his cardiac arrest. Both boys were 14, attended a Christian school, and played basketball. More significantly, both had hundreds of people... including many of you... praying for them. And, incredibly, both made recoveries that their doctors described as miraculous. On this Easter morning, I rejoice that the same power that healed those boys raised Jesus from the grave. "I pray that the eyes of your heart may be enlightened in order that you may know the HOPE to which he has called you, the RICHES of his glorious inheritance in his holy people, and his incomparably great POWER for us who believe. That power is the same as the mighty strength he exerted when he raised Christ from the dead..." (Ephesians 1:18-20). And if any of my dear Facebook friends don't know the true significance of Easter, it is this: (God) has saved us and called us to a holy life – not because of anything we have done but because of his own purpose and grace. This grace was given us in Christ Jesus before the beginning of time, but it has now been revealed through the appearing of our Savior, Christ Jesus, who has destroyed death and has brought life and immortality to light through the gospel (2 Timothy 1:9-10). Happy Easter, my friends. HE IS RISEN!

Even while Christian was still in the hospital, I had friends tell me that I should write a book about his experiences. I easily pooh-poohed the first couple of suggestions. Even though my college degree is in journalism, I've always preferred writing short stories to longer pieces. But when one friend, whom I know is keenly attuned to God, told me that I should consider writing a book, I knew that I needed to seriously consider it.

Still, I dragged my heels. I could easily envision his story compacted into a magazine article that hit the highlights of his miracle, but even as I write this, I struggle to understand why people would want to read all the details. Yet another friend came through with a timely message when she said that people need to hear Christian's story to give them hope.

So, with great reluctance, I started writing this book six months after Christian's cardiac arrest. I've taken the advice of yet another friend who encouraged me to "just start writing and see what comes out." Ironically, not one word of it has been written during daylight hours. I've only worked on it in the middle of the night when I couldn't sleep. For months, I didn't tell anyone, including my husband, that I was working on it. As it nears completion, Christian still doesn't know. I have no idea if anyone outside of my family will ever see this account, but I know that I have been obedient.

Part of why I share Christian's miracle is because of Revelation 19:10, which says, "The testimony of Jesus is the spirit of prophecy." In other words, as we tell and retell Christian's story, it creates an atmosphere where the Lord is invited to work even more miracles. One of my friends interprets that passage to mean simply, "Do it again, Lord." Our family is nothing special, and if God is willing to move so amazingly for us, He is most certainly capable of doing it for others.

The other Scripture verse that stood out to me during Christian's convalescence was John 11:4, which states, "This sickness will not end in death. No, it is for God's glory so that God's Son may be glorified through it." So, I figure that the more Christian's story is shared, the more glory the Lord will receive.

I still can't sing any songs that mention "the name of Jesus" without crying or being overcome with awe at God's power. While much prayer was needed for other aspects of Christian's recovery, we firmly believe that his brain damage was completely healed when we simply anointed him with oil and called on the name of Jesus. It's hard to believe that something so simple can make such a huge difference in a person's life.

The remaining six weeks of Christian's freshman year included a small part in the school musical, *The Music Man*. He had missed more school in one year than was legally allowed, so John and I had to submit a request to the school board to allow him to remain in school. His grades remained remarkably consistent with what they had been before the cardiac arrest. I was gratefully aware that Christian could easily have needed to repeat ninth grade, and he joyfully celebrated the end of the school year with a few buddies at a local fishing lake.

The summer flew by even faster than normal. Christian spent a week at church camp, a week in New York City on a family vacation, and a week in Virginia on a mission trip with our church youth group. But sprinkled in amidst the other activities were plans for The Party. As soon as Christian was discharged from the hospital, I had offered to make good on my promise to throw him the biggest party he'd ever had. But he had deferred, preferring to schedule the party during the summer so guests could play outdoors.

I had to gulp big when Christian wanted to invite all his classmates, church friends, and soccer teammates, but, fortunately for my food budget and parking situation, several were unable to come, so we had a large but manageable crowd. And they were all good kids. The crew enjoyed volleyball, spikeball, cornhole, a campfire, and a movie under the stars, projected onto the side of our house. But the part of the day I cherished most was the homemade slip and slide. I had harbored some concerns that Christian would be too self-conscious about the defibrillator, clearly visible underneath his skin, to go shirtless in public.

It was pure joy to watch him take headlong diving leaps onto the slip and slide with abandon, not caring one whit about the device. I had heard a radio broadcast somewhere around the time he received the implant that essentially said, "Jesus didn't hide his scars. They tell a story of life and love." And I had encouraged Christian to look at his scars the same way. They are evidence that God loved him enough to restore his life.

In the end, I had no regrets about my impulsive offer to throw Christian his biggest party ever. His life was worth celebrating.

Christian takes a flying leap on the home-
made slip and slide at his belated 15th birth-
day celebration. His implanted defibrillator
is visible under the skin on his side.

Christian's party was the last hurrah of the summer because soccer conditioning began the next week. We knew from past years how grueling the workouts would be. Even though the surgeon had absolutely, positively assured us that there was no way Christian's heart rate could get high enough just from exercise to trigger his defibrillator, we all knew that conditioning would test his limits more than any of his other activities. I never let on that I was a little nervous on the first day of conditioning, but I said extra prayers that morning. And I was relieved afterward that he seemed quite normal. When I casually asked later that day if he'd had any issues at all with the defibrillator, he said no. And that was the end of that. I never worried about him accidentally shocking himself again.

The weekend before school starts, Christian's school always participates in a preseason soccer tournament, which draws teams from across our region. That year, the highlight of the entire tournament, for me, occurred off the field. John and Christian were talking on the sidelines between games when a gentleman approached them. Noting the school's name on Christian's jersey, he said he knew that a player from our team had been gravely sick at the previous season's year-end soccer tournament, and he wanted to know how he was doing. Of all the players on Christian's team, this man had no idea that he just happened to ask the player in question.

Christian politely answered the man, but since he still didn't like to talk about the experience, he rather quickly excused himself. John continued talking to the man at length and discovered he had been faithfully praying for Christian for the past ten months! He had attended the coaches' meeting at the fall soccer tournament and when the teams were asked to pray for Christian, he took it to heart. He shared Scriptures with John that he had prayed over Christian, and said he'd called the school three times to get updates on him. What a blessing he was to us! And how humbling. He certainly set an example for us on what it means to commit to pray for someone.

As the soccer season rolled on through the fall, we were approaching the first anniversary of Christian's cardiac arrest. We knew we wanted to do something to mark the occasion, and after much prayer and contemplation, we hit on a fitting way. But we couldn't do it exactly on October 24, when we would've liked to, because Christian would be away at the soccer tournament that he'd missed the year before. But we made all the arrangements to do it the following week.

I completely dreaded October 24. If I could have, I would simply have eliminated it from the calendar that year. Even though we'd been blessed with a wonderfully miraculous outcome, I just really didn't want to be reminded of the horror of the day Christian collapsed. Ironically, I got blindsided the day before. The team always leaves for the soccer tournament on a Wednesday. So, even though the date was October 23, Christian was going through all the same preparations that he'd done the previous year on October 24. I know there was no logical reason for me to be uneasy, but as Christian completed each step of his morning routine, I was silently thankful. I was 100% aware that he was completing tasks he hadn't gotten to do the year before; and I was fully aware of the timeline, remembering what had been happening each moment a year ago.

When he finally got on the bus that morning, I breathed a sigh of relief. And I wasn't alone. Christian's bus driver, who is a dear friend, also drives the team bus to the tournaments. She was feeling the weight of the day right along with me. She told me later that morning how happy she was that day to see Christian waiting at his stop, and she even posted a beautiful tribute on Facebook that gave God all the praise for Christian's recovery. It soothed my soul that she'd remembered, without anyone reminding her.

O nce the trauma of reliving that day was over, October 24 was anticlimactic. It wasn't painful at all, and John and I were happy to buy pizza for the whole soccer team as our way of celebrating Christian's life and thanking them for all their support the previous year. But it was not lost on me that if the Lord hadn't supernaturally interceded for Christian, John and I would have been spending the day very differently... visiting a cemetery.

When John and I had realized that we would be able to attend the soccer tournament, we'd contacted its organizer to ask if we could speak briefly at the coaches' meeting to thank them for all their prayers and share the good news of Christian's recovery. Instead, he kindly invited us to share a ten-minute testimony with all the coaches and players! Having never attended the tournament before, we didn't know that on the last night, there was an optional get-together for all the soccer and volleyball teams at the tournament. We wanted to jump at the opportunity, but we needed to talk to Christian about it first. Since he still didn't like to talk about the incident, we weren't sure how he'd feel about listening to us describe it. In the end, he was agreeable to listening if we just didn't point him out to the entire group. And that was a compromise to which we could easily agree.

John and I had the typical jitters that people get before speaking to a large group, but overall, we were confident that the Lord had provided the opportunity for us, and we were eager to give Him glory for all He had done to heal Christian. When we discuss Christian's story, we try to be sensitive to those whose loved ones may not have experienced miraculous healing. We have no idea why we were so blessed when others are not, but we know for certain that it's not because we are better people or closer to God than others. Only the Lord knows why Christian was spared. But we do believe that God has big plans for Christian's life.

After we shared that night, a woman immediately sought us out. She said she'd been a cardiac nurse for 20 years. She said that as she listened to us describe what happened and how long it took for Christian to receive medical help, she was just waiting for us to say that he had died. She was incredulous that he not only survived but that he did so without any brain damage. Over and over, she repeated, "It's just unheard of." It was reassuring for John and me that someone intimately familiar with cardiac care also recognized Christian's story as a miracle.

Six days after the first anniversary of the cardiac arrest, our family was finally able to celebrate the occasion in the best way we could think of: by serving a free meal to the families of children who were patients in Children's Hospital's PICU. We remembered so clearly the financial hardship many parents faced simply in getting meals while their children were sick. But mostly we wanted to give them hope. We wanted them to know that we'd been exactly where they were the year before and to see with their own eyes how healthy Christian was now.

We were excited to be able to encourage these families, but the details proved a bit trickier than we expected. We had planned to simply order serving pans full of ready-to-eat foods from our local grocer... until we got the price list and went into shock. But, as always, God provided. John remembered a former co-worker who had opened a catering business and who had closely followed Christian's journey while in the hospital. When we contacted him, he readily agreed to help us. When we told him the amount we were able to spend, he said he could put together a nice meal of chicken, cheesy potatoes, green beans almandine, garden salad, rolls, cake, and water. The ingredients cost pretty much all that we could afford, but he graciously waived his profit "for such a good cause."

We also made a couple of encouraging posters for the occasion. One of them quoted 2 Corinthians 1:3-4, "Praise be to the God and Father of our Lord Jesus Christ, the Father of compassion and the God of all comfort, who comforts us in all our troubles, so that we can comfort those in any trouble with the comfort we ourselves receive from God."

The other poster proclaimed, "May the God of hope fill you with all joy and peace as you trust in him, so that you may overflow with hope by the power of the Holy Spirit," from Romans 15:13.

We were happy when one of our closest friends, who had walked through the whole ordeal with us the year before, invited herself to join us in serving the meal. As the families ate in the PICU lounge area, she and John and I mixed and mingled and listened. We were blessed to be able to pray with some families, and always our joy was to share snippets of Christian's story and give them hope for their children. After hearing Christian's story, one fellow believer excused herself quickly to go and anoint her grandson with oil, the same way we had been instructed to do a year earlier.

Christian felt a bit self-conscious throughout the evening, but he served willingly with his characteristic grin. He parked himself near the cake and dished out generous pieces to all comers. He also joined in prayer for some of the families as we ministered to them. In one year, he had come full circle, from being a patient in the PICU to serving there. The message we selected to have written in icing on the cake was the purpose of our being there that night. It was the reason we share Christian's story every chance we get, and it is the reason for this book.

The cake's icing boldly proclaimed, "With God, all things are possible."

Christian praying with a family whose child
was in the same unit he had been in a year
earlier.

Christian was all smiles when we returned to Children's
Hospital a year after the cardiac arrest to serve a meal
to families with loved ones in the Pediatric Intensive Care
Unit.

Epilogue

On June 4, 2022, Christian graduated with high honors from Portersville Christian School without having any more cardiac incidents. He made the most of his senior year of high school, serving as co-captain of the soccer, basketball, and volleyball teams. In soccer, Christian was named Most Valuable Player of his team as well as the entire league. In basketball, he shattered school records in blocked shots, and finished the season at Number Ten in MaxPrep's nationwide standings. He helped make history by playing on his school's first-ever boys' volleyball team.

Christian earned admission to the National Honor Society. Although doctors expected him to have permanent brain damage, God had other plans.

He also appeared in the school musical, *Cinderella*, where he added waltzing to his bag of tricks. Additionally, his peers crowned him Prom King and awarded him a scholarship for leadership.

The mission trip that Christian took to his beloved Dominican Republic right after his cardiac arrest turned out to be his last opportunity during high school, as COVID-19 forced the cancellation of the trips for the next three years. However, he thoroughly enjoyed his senior mission trip to Savannah, Georgia, and just completed another mission trip to West Virginia with his church youth group.

Christian continues to referee soccer games and do landscaping work.

He plans to attend Geneva College in Beaver Falls, Pennsylvania, to major in business management.

Marcia, Christian, and John, after the worst had passed.

Bonus Material

Bonus material can be found via the QR code below or by visiting **www.linktr.ee/heartbeatfromheaven**. There you'll find more information on topics that include:

- Sudden cardiac arrest and steps you can take to protect your child
- A way to find peace with God
- A playlist of the songs mentioned in this book
- CPR classes
- How to contact the author

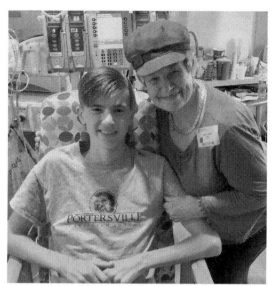

Christian with his adopted grandma, Esther
Taylor, who saw the angel over his head
when we were praying over him.

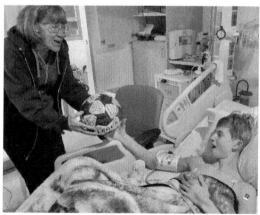

Christian's first glimpse of the soccer ball
that was signed by those who attended a
prayer vigil for him at our church.

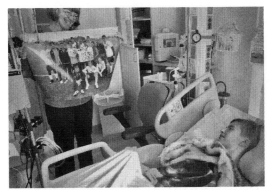

Christian with a poster of his soccer team, taken at the tournament that he missed. It held a prominent spot in every room he had, and was a great conversation starter for all medical personnel who worked with him.

One of the cheerful and inspirational posters that Christian's schoolmates created to brighten up his room.

Made in the USA
Middletown, DE
02 September 2022

73041569R00082